Hangi *and* Hangmen at Usk Prison

A Cautionary Tale

Godfrey Brangham

For Matt who likes facts!

*'Punishment is the way in which society expresses its denunciation of
wrong doing: and in order to maintain respect for law it is essential
that the punishment inflicted for grave crimes should adequately reflect
the revulsion felt by the great majority of citizens for them.'*
Lord Denning

Old Bakehouse Publications

Abertillery

First published in October 2008

ISBN 978-1-905967-14-8

Published in the U.K. by
Old Bakehouse Publications
Church Street,
Abertillery, Gwent NP13 1EA
Telephone: 01495 212600 Fax: 01495 216222
Email: theoldbakeprint@btconnect.com
Website: www.oldbakehouseprint.co.uk

Made and printed in the UK
by J.R. Davies (Printers) Ltd.

British Library Cataloguing in Publication Data: a catalogue
record for this book is available from the British Library.

Contents

Introduction

Murder! Murder! This shrill, piercing cry has long echoed down the ages, yet this most heinous of crimes has elicited a paradoxical reaction in the public at large. On the one hand there is the natural revulsion at such a brutal act whilst on the other it arouses a peculiarly macabre interest. Although those who commit murder form only an infinitesimal percentage of the population, it is strange that even in the public domain such phrases as 'if looks could kill' or 'I could murder a cup of tea' have passed into common usage. History has also shown that murderers and their victims become somehow entwined in a deathly embrace, almost like Siamese twins, the one cannot exist without the other, and there they remain locked together in eternity.

To the devotees of real-life crime it has been a matter of some debate as to why the scale of savagery of individual murders seems to have little bearing on whether they are remembered in the years, decades or centuries following their commitment. It is indeed an indisputable fact that they exert a peculiar hold on the public imagination, what could be termed the 'fascination of the ugly', perhaps because the perpetrators are so utterly alien to ourselves. This fascination not only encompasses true crime but spills over into the realms of fiction. Detective novels, especially those by such illustrious authors as Agatha Christie, Ngaio Marsh, P.D. James and a host of others, are still amongst the most popular of literary genres. Television consistently broadcasts detective cum murder mysteries, making household names of such figures as Morse, Frost, Jane Tennison, along with a series of American based programmes; CSI, Columbo, Perry Mason, Criminal Intent, being only a few of innumerable titles.

This attraction to the seamier side of life was well illustrated a little while ago when a friend complained to me about his elderly aunt. Each Sunday she would disappear behind the pages of one of the tabloids from which would issue various oaths and admonishments, the commonest being, 'this is disgusting!', or 'how can they print such things!'. Yet every Sunday morning as he was leaving for the newsagents she would shout after him, 'Don't forget my paper!'

A murder trial, unlike those for more minor offences, always attracts attention though perhaps more so in the past when a guilty verdict would mean donning the 'black cap' and sentencing the prisoner to death. The proceedings of such a trial are enacted in high drama; the conflicts that arise in interpreting the evidence, the ingenuity of the prosecution and defence counsels, the input by forensic pathologists, the lone figure in the dock, and the calm aura of the presiding Judge. Then finally the rising tension as the jury returns and delivers its verdict. High drama indeed!

The most infamous of British murderers was of course Jack the Ripper who plied his grisly trade in the east end of London well over 100 years ago, yet the books devoted to him, and more particularly the many theories relating to his true identity, continue unabated to this present day. To an extent the Whitechapel murders have coloured our thinking of those times as murders involving such extremes of violence were in fact quite rare, whereas poison was the most common method employed.

Another legend in the gallery of murderers was Dr Hawley Harvey Crippen, a mild mannered

Dr Hawley Harvey Crippen.

4

insignificant little man who killed his wife, buried some of her remains in the cellar of their home, subsequently arrested, tried at the Old Bailey, found guilty and hanged in 1911. A simple enough everyday type of murder, yet his fame persists even to the extent of being accorded both a film and a successful stage musical!

In America, where today murders occur at a rate of one every 20 minutes, the extraordinary case of Lizzie Borden still holds pride of place. This young lady in the summer of 1888 attacked and killed her parents with an axe. In one of the most incomprehensible decisions ever made by a jury she was found 'Not Guilty'. As a child I distinctly remember chanting a ditty about her, though just as with Georgy Porgy, we didn't fully understand the meaning of the words we so glibly recited in the playground. It went like this:

Lizzie Borden's axe.

Lizzie Borden.

Lizzie Borden took an axe and gave her mother forty wacks
When she saw what she had done, she gave her father forty-one.

It is truly odd that the most grisly murders can engender such things. In this country over the past 150 years there have been committed literally hundreds of the most foul killings, yet outside of Jack the Ripper, Crippen and perhaps John Christie the majority have slowly become lost in the mists of time, only aficionados of the genre retaining a knowledge and interest in them. Who today remembers the great poisoners such as Pritchard, Lamson, and Neil Cream, or the callous Dr Buck Ruxton who in the thirties dismembered both his wife and maidservant wrapping them in newspaper and throwing their various parts into a river some hundred or so miles from his home in Lancaster. Again those mysterious, unknown poets rose to the occasion and composed the following lyrics to the refrain of 'Red Sails in the Sunset':

Dr Buck Ruxton.

Red stains on the carpet,
Red stains on the knife,
Oh, Dr Buck Ruxton you cut up your wife,
The nursemaid, she saw you, and threatened to tell,
So, Dr Buck Ruxton, you killed her as well.

Capital punishment has had of course its adherents and its objectors; both sharply divided, both passionate and sincere in their views. In 1948 this provocative issue had engendered evermore controversy; the Commons having voted for abolition whilst the Lords had overruled it. During this interim period those found guilty of murder had their sentences commuted to life imprisonment. After the pro-hanging decision by the House of Lords the practice of executing murderers was resumed. Since 1964 the opponents have won the day and murders are no longer punishable by hanging in the United Kingdom. Two famous authors of the Victorian period, when public hangings were common before 1868, waxed lyrical, though in an abhorrent tone, on the subject. Charles Dickens, one of the greatest writers in the English language provides this graphic description of the time that he witnessed such a hanging:

'I was purposely, on the spot, from midnight of the night before; and was a near witness of the whole process of the building of the scaffold, the gathering of the crowd the gradual swelling of the concourse with the coming-on of the day, the hanging of the man, the cutting of the body down, and the removal of it into the prison. From the moment of my arrival, when there were but a few small boys in the street, and all those young thieves, and all clustered together behind the barriers nearest the drop - down to the time when I saw the body with its dangling head, being carried on a wooden bier into the gaol - I did not see one token in all the immense crowd; at the windows, in the streets, on the house-tops, anywhere: of any one emotion suitable to the occasion. No sorrow, no salutary terror, no abhorrence, no seriousness; nothing but ribaldry, debauchery, levity, drunkenness and flaunting vice in fifty other shapes.'

Oddly enough William Makepeace Thackeray was also present at the same hanging, and took up his pen to write the following:

'I feel myself ashamed and degraded at the brutal curiosity which took me to that brutal sight …. It seems to me that I had been abetting an act of frightful wickedness …. I came away that morning with a disgust for murder, but it was for the murder that I saw done.'

Another Victorian writer George Gissing took a slightly different viewpoint when a character in his novel 'New Grub Street' commented:

'A man who comes to be hanged has the satisfaction of knowing that he has just brought society to its last resource. He is a man of such fatal importance that nothing will serve against him but the supreme effort of law. In a way, you know, that is success.'

The murder cases described in this book took place between 1874 and 1922 and whilst the integrity and administrative structure of the judiciary system was of a high standard, well admired and thus copied by many other countries, they were at one great disadvantage in that forensic science was only at its rudimentary stage. It may be that those intent on committing the ultimate crime frequently resorted to the use of poison, this perhaps being the 'safer' means of disposing of the intended victim. However the cases here are not of that order, they were simply brutal and violent. There exists of course a certain nostalgia for the late Victorian era perhaps encouraged by Conan Doyles' tales of Sherlock Holmes, where villains (the word criminal is all together too modern!), carried out their nefarious deeds undercover of fog bound alleyways and naphtha-lit gloomy squares, where frock-coated men hovered in the background and menace suffused the very blackness of the night.

Murders in Victorian times usually belong to one of three categories; by stabbing, by poisoning, or by strangulation, although drowning also had its adherents! Perhaps poisoning could be viewed as the most callous means of taking a life, as besides being coldly premeditated, the victim who must have not only been familiar but close to the perpetrator, often suffered horrendous pain, violent muscle spasms, dying eventually in the throes of agony.

One well-known feature of the human psyche is that apparently incontrovertible facts are often questioned with regard to their veracity by a small number of individuals. There are numerous examples of this phenomenon; today we have the many alternative theories as to how Princess Diana died, did Lee Harvey Oswald really shoot President Kennedy, did aliens actually land at Roswell? There are even those who believe that the moonlandings were faked by Hollywood!

Naturally reading a book devoted to violent crime has its own psychological slant, which can vary from the prosaic quest for knowledge to the more basic desire for diversion and entertainment. Here, certainly in the case of Joseph Garcia, you are being asked to be both armchair detective, and 'judge and jury'. Of course in the intervening years the emotional dust has settled and time itself has tended to obscure some of the details of the crimes. Thus my aim is a simple one. To present to you the background and known facts of the crimes, and in the case of the Llangibby murders that you yourselves may judge whether all those years ago there was indeed a miscarriage of justice.

However before we meet Mr Garcia there is a section on the historical development of the prison systems in Usk, which began at the Castle Keep and ended with today's prison in Maryport Street. The conditions and sentences undergone by the poor wretches who were imprisoned in the Bridewell or later the House of Correction was truly shocking. It does however offer a salutory lesson in what is or isn't acceptable, although there are many today who believe with some justification that the pendulum has swung the other way and sentences are often too light.

The final section deals with those men who were employed to carry out the wishes of the state - the executioners. Oddly all were from the northern part of England, all could be termed working class and all attempted to carry out their macabre work with due pride and efficiency.

PART ONE

A Brief History of Usk Prisons

*　　*　　*

Chapter One
Bridewell and the Houses of Correction

On the merely superficial level the purpose of imprisonment seems plain enough, to incarcerate dangerous people, to punish those who commit crimes and, almost as an afterthought, to reform. The essence that comes down the years from the seventeenth to the mid-nineteenth century prisons is one of unremitting suffering, wretchedness in the extreme, and untold misery and pain. In addition a public almost totally ignorant of this state of affairs.

Usk Prison today.

It is ironic that the small picturesque town of Usk set as it is in an idyllic rural area of Monmouthshire has for hundreds of years held within its boundaries a prison - today the county gaol.

This grey granite-faced building stands only a few hundred yards from a similar grey-stoned structure, the ancient church of St Mary's. A place of repentance staring uneasily across the fields to that of retribution.

St. Mary's.

The present gaol in Maryport Street was built in the 1840s but Usk's historical connection with such institutions goes back much further. Originally called Houses of Correction they were set up in the seventeenth century, their purpose not so much for punishment but merely to remove from society those who had become nuisances to the local population. They were termed idlers and mainly consisted of 'vagabonds, rogues and beggars', in short, the general riff-raff of the time. It was believed that by subjecting this amorphous group to a regime of strictness and discipline it would eventually pay dividends and see them become more useful members of society. Naturally those who refused to cooperate received extremely harsh punishments.

A law was passed in 1609 that forced all counties in England to have their own Houses of Correction under the control of Justices of the Peace who in turn reported to the Quarter Sessions held in each county. Although these measures quickly established a structured approach to the problem, it is easy to surmise that there would be little consistency in the length of 'sentences' imposed between the differing counties, the space available being the main denominator.

Unfortunately an increasing tide of criminal behaviour soon became instrumental in changing the philosophy of these institutions as they slowly began to resemble what today would be regarded as places of imprisonment. However those so punished were in fact usually guilty of quite minor misdemeanours, drunk and disorderly behaviour, petty thieving, verbal abuse and prostitution being the most common indictments. Thus by the late eighteenth century this system of confinement had become well established throughout the country, and can be viewed as the precursor of today's practices.

The Houses of Correction were known as Bridewells; this name arising from the Palace of Bridewell which stood on the western bank of Fleet River the area between the Thames and present-day Fleet Street. The palace being a huge and spacious complex built during the reign of Henry VIII was used to entertain and hold foreign monarchs and for nearly a decade leased by the French Ambassador. However by 1550 it had undergone a complete reversal of roles and was now given over to the relief of the poor. Many such had migrated from the countryside thus dramatically swelling the numbers in need of aid. Amongst them were gangs of thieves and hoodlums who soon became a real threat to law and order in the capital.

Thus Bridewell was not only a refuge for the poor but also a place of incarceration for criminals. The latter were forced to carry out menial tasks including the cleaning of the sewers after first receiving twelve lashes of the whip. Although the exact date is unknown, in Usk a similar Bridewell institution was built on a site adjoining a medieval hospital, being first recorded in the 1630 *Town Survey of Usk*. This House of Correction was under

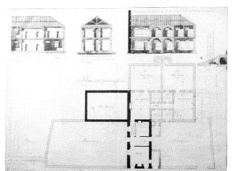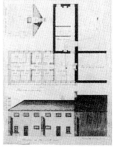

Architectural Drawing of Usk House of Correction.

the control of the Portreeve who had the responsibility of appointing Bridewell Keepers. It is easy to envisage the squalid conditions that existed in such a place, where the distinctly hostile environment affected not only the health of the incumbents but also the keepers. Taking an alternative viewpoint, it might also have deterred people from breaking the law so avoiding incarceration there! During the Civil War the prison population rapidly expanded so a second building in Bridge Street, today known as Gordon House, was commandeered.

In *A History of Monmouthshire Vol 3 Part 1* Joseph Bradney refers to a report by John Howard the philanthropist entitled *The State of the Prisons*. He had undertaken a tour of England and Wales in 1777 visiting each House of Correction.

County Bridewell at Usk

This prison was formerly a chapel. On the ground floor is a room for men and another for women. There are two more rooms at the top of the house, but I saw no prisoners there. The keeper's wife told me that many years ago the prison was crowded and herself, her father (who was then keeper) and many others of the family had the gaol-fever, three of them and several prisoners died of it. The danger of such a calamity in the future would be much lessened if proper rooms were built in the keeper's large garden. The rooms which were building in 1779 will be some small improvement to this prison. There is a court with a pump. The prisoners have some allowance. The spinning wheels are not provided by the county. The keeper has all profit of the work.

Salary £20 – fees 5s 6d
1774 Aug. 21, prisoners 2. 1776 Sept. 6, prisoners 3. 1779 June 8,
prisoners 7.

Gaol fever was in fact typhus - a bacterial infection spread by the bites of lice and fleas. Its symptoms were severe headache, high fever, muscle pains, a red rash with eventual delirium and death.

Site of House of Correction, Bridge Street, Usk.

The keeper and his wife referred to by John Howard was almost certainly John and Elizabeth Watkins, he dying in 1778 with his widow continuing in the job for another year before a David Lewis took over. The poverty of the prisoners was to an extent relieved in November 1778 by the Justices of the Peace directing that five pounds five shillings be allotted for the provision of adequate clothing for them. The following year they agreed that four pair of shoes should be allowed the convicts.

Iron bars of the House of Correction, Bridge Street, Usk.

Indeed the poorer people in the community were gradually accruing such debts that the numbers held in Usk's Bridewell inevitably increased. The harsh conditions they experienced there often led to either a slow death by starvation or to the equally pernicious gaol fever. In contrast, those convicted as 'criminals' ended up in the county gaol at Monmouth.

For most of the eighteenth century those imprisoned simply idled their time away each day as boring as the next. This state of affairs underwent a dramatic change in the early 1780s when it occurred to the powers that be that convicts might prove useful by employing them to undertake 'desirable' tasks which would be helpful to the county. Of course education, the teaching of a trade or any attempt at rehabilitation was not yet envisaged, indeed most of the free population were not educated or skilled. The reality was that with the dramatic rise in the population of the country these Houses of Correction, which had been around for nigh on three hundred years were no longer able to cope. The politicians of the day were now forced by public concern to address the problem, as crime not always of a petty nature was likewise on the increase.

With the coming of the Victorian age the annual crime rate of 5,000 went inexorably upwards until by 1840 it had reached 20,000! The overriding populous opinion was that these criminals should be justly punished, but what actual form should that take? The prisons in 1800 were generally not large enough to accommodate such intakes and in addition were generally old and delapidated. Transportation to Australia was one method of removing such individuals from British society, whilst hundreds were permanently silenced by execution, the high rate due to the remarkable number of offences carrying the death penalty. The population in Monmouthshire in 1801 was approaching 50,000 yet within half a century this figure was to exceed 100,000. The incidence of crime in the county duly followed this trend so that there was a real fear of social breakdown occurring.

The Minutes of the Monmouthshire Quarter Sessions of August 1810 show that the Justices of the Peace were directed to make alterations to the House of Correction to ensure that it was suitable to receive lunatics. For some reason these instructions were never acted upon for in 1814 the building was auctioned to a Philip Richards, who some nine years later made a handsome profit by reselling the property back as a House of Correction for £1,000. The premises were now too small to accommodate the growth in numbers of detainees so extensive alterations were carried out by James Maddox and his son George. On completion new workshop equipment was installed, including spinning wheels for the females and a machine to produce flour. By the end of 1821 all was ready for the influx of new prisoners under the keeper John George.

The next addition to the building took place in 1824 with the installation in the front yard of the infamous tread wheel or tread mill as it was called at the time. The first use of the wheel occurred on 3rd September 1824 when it was stipulated that the maximum time spent on the wheel by a prisoner should not exceed fifteen minutes for each session. No female prisoner took part in this gruelling activity. As can be imagined this particular 'exercise' was not very popular and a number of inmates refused to cooperate, however after due sanctions were levied they changed their minds! In fact the Justices themselves showed concern over the effects of the wheel and insisted that prisoners received adequate care when resting from the treading the wheel.

Escapes from the House of Correction were on the whole rare, however on 26th May 1823 four men got away, whilst a female prisoner Margaret Munkley also managed the same feat in June 1824 but was quickly recaptured. Those who made unsuccessful bids for freedom were punished by being placed in the 'dark' cell. To contemporary eyes the sentences handed down for the various misdemeanours often appear harsh and occasionally iniquitous. Fortunately the Keepers Book of the old House of Correction for 1821 - 1834 has been preserved and is currently held at Gwent Records Office. Though many of the convictions were for debt, from the hundreds within its covers I have selected a few illustrative examples of the less common 'deeds':

> *1st December 1821: Received the body of James Smith charged with being a rogue and vagabond for that he did wander abroad as a petty Chapman and Pedlar, offering for sale goods and merchandizes not being duly licensed. To be imprisoned for one month.*

11th January 1822: Received the body of Mary Howard charged upon oath of William Watkins ...with having been delivered of a Bastard Child in the said parish of Llanfoist. To be imprisoned and kept to hard labour for the space of one whole year.

28th January 1822: Received the body of William Matthews charged with having used a hook for the destruction of salmon in the River Usk. To be imprisoned for two months.

28th September 1827: Received the body of James Williams charged with stealing three cabbages cultivated and used for the food of beasts growing in a field in the occupation of Messrs Wheely and Morgan. To be imprisoned and kept to hard labour for the space of three months.

26th January 1832: Received Richard Powell of the parish of Llangibby being an Idle and Disorderly person ... has wilfully refused and neglected his said family. To be imprisoned and kept to hard labour for the space of one month.

7th July 1832: Received William Morgan who unlawfully and maliciously destroyed and damaged with intent to destroy one chestnut tree and one gooseberry tree in a certain garden ... To be imprisoned and kept to hard labour for one Calendar Month.

12th August 1832: Received Thomas Jones charged and convicted as a rogue and vagabond who did play in a public road with a Thimble Table being an instrument of gaming and a game of chance. To be imprisoned and kept to hard labour for the space of two Calendar Months.

Other entries relate to the general running of the gaol.

26th November 1821: Mr George to procure for Rees Howell (quite naked) one common pair of trousers and one flannel jacket.

28th October 1830: The gaoler is desired to change the prisoners allowance of food per day according to the following scale as is practicable - one and half lbs of best wheaten bread; one lb potatoes; quarter of a pound of oatmeal; salt as required.

Chapter Two
A New Gaol

By the 1830s the building of new and much larger prisons had become a country-wide priority, although wherever possible the old Houses of Correction were to be enlarged and updated. The general opinion was that those incarcerated should face tough daily regimes in the belief that these would act as a deterrent against committing future crimes. These criteria were now being considered both in Parliament and by those directly involved in crime and punishment. In line with this rationale, the Quarter Sessions of Monmouthshire for 2nd September 1839 took the decisive line of appointing a Committee of Magistrates to investigate all aspects of the problem, with William Adam Williams in the chair.

They soon came to realise that the old House of Correction in Usk, and indeed the County Gaol at Monmouth were unable to cope with the high level of convictions for criminal activities. When the committee reported back on 23rd April 1840 they firstly emphasised the need for a new House of Correction and in addition offered three possible systems of management of such a prison.

Plan A was the 'Silent Rule' whereby prisoners would not be allowed to speak to each other. Besides being unnatural and quite alien to normal human behaviour it was also the most difficult to supervise and enforce. In fact it could be argued that it would inevitably exacerbate trickery and deceptions by the prisoners and prove counter-productive to their rehabilitation.

Plan B was the 'Separation Rule'. This arose from the genuine concerns of the clergy, politicians and philanthropists that the close nature of prisoners lives could lead to promiscuity and the eventual decline in their moral and spiritual well-being. However the solitary confinement of prisoners to dark flea-ridden cells for sometimes weeks or months at the time might easily engender mental deterioration.

Silent and Separate Rule.

Plan C was a combination of A and B with all its attendant drawbacks. As can be seen below it was this plan that was eventually implemented!

Their report included a possible location for the building being a meadow owned by Mr Davies of Cwrt-y-Gollen. They stated that:

> ' ...the New House of Correction be adapted for the safe custody and confinement of 90 males and 30 females in a manner proposed in the above resolution. That the Plan C modified in pursuant of the last resolution in regard to the larger number of prisoners be adopted. That Mr Thomas H. Wyatt be appointed the architect for the New House of Correction. That the Committee shall have the power to perfect the purchase of the field belonging to Mr Davies. That a Committee shall have power to draw on the

County Treasurer to such sums as may appear necessary for the carrying on of the work which in whole shall not exceed £16,000. But it appears probable that £3,500 will be required for the purchase of land and other expenses connected with the erection of the New House of Correction previous to the thirtieth day of March next. That the sum be defrayed by rates necessary for the raising such sums. That the remaining £12,500 to be expended on this object shall be raised by loan ...'

It transpired that the amount required was obtained on the basis of a mortgage loan from three London businessmen. The County Rates realised the rest. Tenders were now sent out for the actual building materials, the successful offer for providing the stone being made by Llanbradach Quarry at a price of one shilling and seven and a half pence per yard. Messrs James by April 1841 reported that the laying of the foundations was going according to plan, whilst Messrs Wilcox & Sons were now almost finished in building a perimeter wall to act as a protection for the many implements and machinery needed to carry out the construction work.

Poor weather in the autumn of 1841 caused some delays to the workforce but by the following summer it could be reported that the governor's residence, the wash-houses, the female quarters and the laundry had all been completed. By the end of the year the exterior structures were finished and the plumbing, glazing and plastering were nearing completion. The entire project was eventually turned over to the authorities in the summer of 1843 some five months after the intended date.

The Pentonville Model

There was increasing resistance from abroad to the transportation of prisoners which coupled with pressure from reformists at home ultimately led to the building of a 'model' prison at Pentonville. The revolutionary design adopted was based on two American penitentiaries, Walnut Street in Philadelphia and Auburn in New York. They were designed on a pentachiron format with a turnkey positioned centrally who would therefore be able to view the entire area. They also pioneered the 'silent' and 'separate' system of managing prisoners. Pentonville adopted both the design and rules of the American system and began operating in 1842 to become the role model for all other prisons in Britain, including the one under construction at Usk.

Of course the 'silent' and 'separate' philosophies were in direct contrast to those of the old Bridewells, where in Usk the prisoners freely mingled in over-crowded rooms. However each of these new rules had their proponents where powerful figures aligned themselves to one side or the other. Governor Chesterton of Pentonville ascribed to the Silent regime and was deeply upset at those who argued against it. In fact to show the negative aspects of the Separate Rule he recounts with obvious relish the effects of eighteen months solitary confinement on prisoners:

'At the expiration of that time, they were transferred to Millbank Prison, where their attenuated condition, and mental disturbance created a sensation in the mind of the then Governor, who could not repress his condemnation of separation to so fatal an extent.'

On the opposite side stood John Clay who claimed that not one case of insanity had resulted from such a type of incarceration and in a number of instances they had actually improved the moral standing of the prisoners during their confinement! The pendulum swung from side to side and as is frequently the case it came to rest in a neutral position so a hybrid of both systems was usually implemented gaining the worst of both worlds.

As can be seen from the photograph Usk was built on the same design as Pentonville with a central hub from which the prison officers could view all wings radiating outwards.

Conditions at the House of Correction

Many of the tasks allotted to the prisoners were in reality merely a means of

Usk Gaol, early 20th century.

filling the passage of time. Often the many tedious and exhausting tasks were carried out within the cells, however three others were performed outside.

The Treadwheel

This contraption had been invented by a civil engineer William Cubitt, and was first employed at Brixton gaol in 1819. The one at Usk had been transferred from the old House of Correction in Bridge Street and later modified. It was comprised of a large drum fitted with parallel lines of slatted steps on which prisoners would rhythmically pace causing the drum to revolve.

Each man (females were exempt from the wheel) was made to step nearly 20,000 feet per day. The wheel was kept in constant motion the prisoners working for 15 minutes followed by a rest period of 5 minutes before resuming. This regime differed slightly from that employed at the old House of Correction where it was 10 minutes on and 10 minutes off and the prisoners all stepping together.

Of course with the Silent Rule in operation the men on the treadwheel were not allowed to communicate with each other. The punishment for breaking this rule would normally consist of a restricted diet and a

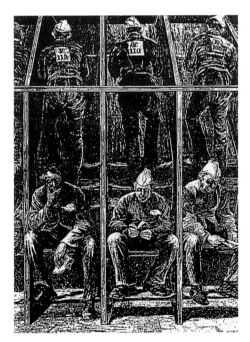

Prisoner at the Tread Wheel.

period spent in what was termed the 'punishment cell'. The wheel remained in use at the gaol until 1901 when it was dismantled and buried beneath what today is the prison sports field.

Stone Breaking

This was normally reserved for those who were sentenced with hard labour or for those who had transgressed the prison rules. This physically arduous task was carried out in specially designed cells where large blocks of stone from local quarries were reduced to chippings using a hand-held sledgehammer. The chippings were intended for use in the construction of new roads. As can be imagined the prisoners employed in this work often sustained injuries to hand and head requiring the attention of the prison medical officer.

Oakum Picking

One of the most hated jobs alloted to prisoners was that of oakum picking. Large disused ropes made of sissal had to be unravelled and picked until the individual fibres were obtained. They would then be cleaned and teased before being used either for mattress filling or sent to boat repair yards where they would be mixed with tar and

Oakum Picking.

applied as a water-proofing material. The hands of the prisoners were frequently stripped raw by this process, but despite this the task was still in use at the beginning of the twentieth century.

Whitewashing

In the early days of Usk gaol the corridors and cells were cast in an almost constant gloom, with candles providing the only source of light. The situation improved slightly in the 1850s when gas lighting came into use but the prison still remained a shadowy place. To help overcome this the whitewashing of all walls was undertaken by the prisoners in order to enhance the amount of reflected light.

Other more minor tasks included tailoring, shoemaking, weaving and rug making. Female prisoners were of course separated from the men and undertook such duties as sewing, cooking for the prison, and working in the laundry. The old system of all prisoners simply milling around in large rooms had now passed as they performed a range of 'worthwhile' duties.

The Prisoner's Diet

The arrival of food was the most eagerly anticipated event of the day. It was served by opening a small aperture or trap in the cell door and thrusting it through, but if the incumbent wasn't ready then it would be wasted. As one prisoner commented, '... *they were thrown on the floor as food might be thrown to a dog, and the door was banged again.*' However in

Prisoners being fed in their cells.

the more sympathetic gaols the cell door was opened to reveal a warder with a large tea urn plus baskets of brown bread.

The quantity and quality of the food was to the prisoner far more important than the method of delivery. This varied from prison to prison, but a typical 'menu' was as follows:

17

Male Prisoners	Female Prisoners
Breakfast	Breakfast
8 oz. bread & 1 pint gruel	*6 oz. bread & 1 pint gruel*
Dinner	Dinner
8 oz. bread	*6 oz. bread*
Supper	Supper
8 oz. bread & 1 pint gruel	*6 oz. bread & 1 pint gruel*

There were fortunately certain variations on this appallingly monotonous diet. As a concession on some Sundays they had cheese added to the supper meal, one ounce for males and three quarters for females. Again if they were imprisoned with hard labour then both males and females were given potatoes, soup and extra cheese on designated days.

Governors and Warders

It would appear, according to a Rev. Daniel Nihill that the personal qualities required in prison officers differed according to whether the particular gaol operated a 'silent' or 'solitary' system of discipline. In the case of the silent system prisoners were often in close contact with each other, therefore the governor and warders needed to be men of exceptional body strength, possess a high degree of courage and an austere, commanding presence, whereas for those institutions that practised a solitary regime this type of person was not crucial. In fact recruitment leaned towards people exhibiting such qualities as integrity, intelligence and Christian ethics. Thus chaplains had a prominent role to play here.

12th Report of Inspectors of Prisons
Southern & Western District Monmouthshire
Usk County House of Correction: Officers Positions & Salaries

Name	Office	Age	Appointment	Salary
John Merrett	Governor	48	1829 Michaelmas	115
Mary Merrett	Matron	42	1829 Michaelmas	30
Charles Mason	Warder	42	1839 April	52
James Boulton	Surgeon	32	1842 Trinity	81
Keynon Homfray	Chaplain	32	1843 April	200
John Brain	Warder	35	1843 Oct	52
Thomas Skipp	Porter	42	1844 Feb	52
Thomas Powell	Schoolmaster	34	1844 May	52
James Green	Warder	47	1846 Sep	52
John Jones	Warder	35	1845 March	52
Mary Phillips	Warder/Schoolmistress	30	1845 July	30
William Prothero	Cook	29	1846 May	52
William Dinham	Warder	22	1846 Sep	52

Chapter Three
A Prisoner's Perspective

The descriptions of the prisons and prison life in the previous chapter have either come from the records of those who staff them, the Governors and warders, or by those who were delegated to inspect such institutions, the Visiting Justices. The information they have thus provided is not necessarily a sanatised account, but it is one that was taken from one perspective only.

They were in a position of power; those in charge ordered, prisoners obeyed. The perception on one side of the 'cell door' greatly differed from that viewed on the other. A simply analogy which illustrates this is when a doctor informs a patient that they have a terminal illness. The doctor's decision is based on diagnosis and clinical observation. For patients the world has catastrophically changed, death is imminent, they are soon to take leave of their relatives, sons, daughters, brothers, sisters. This human trauma is of course felt by the doctors, but however regretful the case, they must move on to the next patient. Perception is different for both.

So it is with the prisoners. Their incarceration obviously affects them more than those who guard them. Obtaining their views is a difficult matter, for not withstanding the long passage of time, the majority of prisoners were illiterate so could not put pen to paper to express and describe their times in such places. Yet we do have one extraordinary document, written by an obviously well

Victorian Male and Female Prisoners.

educated prisoner who chose to remain anonymous. Although the prison described is in fact Pentonville, as Usk was built and run on the same model, there is no reason to believe that Usk prison materially differed. It is a graphic account of the realities of a mid-Victorian prison and as such it gives a vivid but alternative view of the day-to-day life within its grey walls. It is reproduced here exactly as it was set down all those years ago, beginning at the day of admission.

I was ordered to go to the end of the passage, where the principal of the receiving ward was standing. He ordered me to strip and go into a bath down some steps. I obeyed of course; in a very few minutes he called to me and threw me a towel, telling me to dry myself and come out. This too, I did; and on reaching the top of the step leading from the bath, found my clothes had disappeared. There stood the principal however, who whisked the towel out of my hand and threw it away, and told me to stand up, naked as I was.

'Turn around.'
'Lift both legs.'
'Lift the right leg, now the left.'
'Hold up the sole of the foot, now the other.'
'Now stoop. Stand up.'

'Open your mouth.'

'Here take this bundle of clothes and put them on.'

The object of all this examination is that no prisoner should have a chance of concealing anything about his person. I was then called into the room where the doctor was, and here I saw another chief warder. My comb and brushes and toothbrush were set on one side, and my ticket with my name and number placed with them. I begged for the toothbrush.

'If you are particular about your teeth my man,' said the chief warder, 'Use a corner of your towel.'

I was measured in height, in girth of chest, and was weighed. A card was then given to me with a number on it, which I was told was my number, and to which I was always to answer, as prisoners left their names behind them, and were never addressed by them while in prison.

The warder pointed out the way along the passage to a cell, the door of which he opened and introduced me to my lodging under Her Majesty's roof. The little ticket with the number on he took from me, placed it in a rack over the doorway, and shut me in.

When the door of my cell snapped to upon me, I found myself in a dark stone box fourteen feet by seven, with a begrimed window-pane, heavily barred up under the ceiling. There was a row of shining utensils for sanitary, eating and other uses ... the walls were painted yellow up to a certain height and white-washed above that.

The man in the cell above me began to march up and down. I heard each step he took, clanking through the asphalt and iron-ceilinged roof of my cell, till after half an hour, the monotonous tramp, tramp of this restless prisoner struck a chill into my brain, and I hammered on the ceiling of my cell, to make him stop.

It grew dark about eight o'clock in the evening, and the bell rang at that hour for bedtime. I then took down from where it stood upright against the wall of my cell, the wooden plank which was the basis of my bed, laid upon it the hard mattress which was rolled up in the corner under the wooden shelf, and took from their appointed place above the mattress the tightly-rolled sheets and blankets and laid them upon the bed.

Scarcely had I been in bed a few moments, when a banging of the doors of all the cells of the prison startled my overwrought system. This sound grew nearer and nearer, and passed by the critical moment when I thought my own cell had been reached, only to recommence in the far distance and grew louder and nearer once more. The warders were collecting the work done in the cells of the prisoners during the day. This work and the tools with which it is done (be they scissors, needle, thread, or what not), must be placed outside the door of his cell by the prisoner before he settles down for his night's rest.

Waking with an oppresive weight of foul air on one's chest, at 5.45 the prison bell, a squeaky concern, which toils about eighty times, is rung as herald to a day of hard, unremitting and almost unrecompensed work.

I soon grew thin and pale on the prison diet. For breakfast (about 7.45 a.m.) I was given a pint of tea and a six-ounce bread roll; no butter. I then worked and took an hour's exercise, and at 12 midday a tin containing two potatoes and some beans and fat bacon (a gruesome and nauseating mixture, slimy and apt to cause sickness) and a five-ounce brown roll was thrust into my cell. I then worked at sewing sandbags until *five in the evening, when a pint cocoa and an eight-ounce brown roll (dry bread as before) was again thrust into my cell. That was tea and supper combined. I had no more food until 7.45 the next morning. I soon turned into a pale and trembling mortal as a prisoner in Her Majesty's prison. These trembling fits, accompanied by faintness, regularly overtook me about an hour before the next 'meal' was due.*

The prisoner now described in detail the food that he was served each day of the week, varying between a thick, stringy soup, a hideous chunk of putty-like suet, and a tough piece of steak floating in a tin half-filled with gravy. The prisoners were not allowed knives so had to eat with a shallow wooden spoon, using their teeth to tear off bite-size pieces of food. The eventual effect of this 'diet' was to precipitate ever-worsening stomach problems and diarrhoea, to the extent that he was transferred to the hospital wing. He again takes up the story:

But I slept no better at nights, and the reasons for my wakefulness were many. To begin with, I have a horror of vermin, and vermin abounded in the hospital cell. I woke on the first night of my tenancy of this new cell to the dismal sound of cockroaches dropping in great haste and hurry from the ceiling, walls, and wooden sideboard, and it was not long before I felt and found one running nimbly across my face, as I lay, only raised a few inches from the boarded floor on my plank bed.

You grow gradually aware, as the morning draws on, that you are in the midst of a great cesspool. If prisoners were forced to use their pots during the night others soon became aware of the fact. When an occurrence of this kind happens, which owing to the nature of the food, it does very frequently, the fact is made known by the nasal telegram, almost over the whole ward, announcing an addition to the already over-tainted atmosphere.

Although the majority of such prisoners survived their ordeals there were always those of a more fragile nature who became mentally disturbed by the conditions. Their incumbent poverty on the outside of the prison walls offered little relief when they were eventually freed. In fact the following recorded conversation between a prisoner and his visiting wife well illustrates this:

'Why haven't you been here afore to see me?'
    Couldn't.'
    'Why not?'
    'No tin, had to 'ave a whip round amongst 'em all to get up fourpence to pay my railway fare down here today.'
    'Don't believe it.'
    'Ah; it's all very well for you to talk. You 'ave your meal regular now. Well I don't. I've had nothing to eat since yesterday morning. You 'ave. You've something to be thankful for - I 'aven't. Don't you grumble.'

The Cat-O-Nine Tails
For serious misdemeanours by prisoners the usual punishment, besides a reduction in food rations, was to be flogged. The culprit was stripped to the waist and tied by his arms and legs to a triangular structure. Present would be the governor, the prison doctor, and a number of warders one of whom would be carrying a leather cat-o-nine tails. The governor would firstly state the offence and then the required number of lashes to be administered. As each lash caused a weal on the back of

the prisoner the doctor's job was to keep count. Usually there was a scream of pain by the third lash, moaning by the seventh and then silence. If the man lapsed into semi-consciousness the doctor would order one of the warders to throw a bucket of cold water on the wretches back. The shock of this instantly revived the prisoner and the flogging could be continued until the agreed number of lashes had been administered.

Awaiting flogging with the Cat-o-nine tails!

On being carried back to his cell the punished individual would have an ointment and bandages applied under the supervision of the very same doctor who had attended his flogging. The warder who had wielded the cat-o-nine tails received an extra payment for his labours. Although this punishment was normally carried out in a private area of the prison, the cries and screams of the person being flogged echoed along the corridors and into each cell, thus acting as a deterrent to others.

Cat-o-nine tails!

The unremitting squalor of their lives, the hopelessness of the future pushed some of the incumbents to contemplate 'ending it all.' Of course suicide in those days was a criminal offence so the attempt had to be successful or they would end up with even longer sentences. The most popular method was simply to hurl oneself from the top verandah on to the stone floors below. The prison authorities were naturally well aware of this, their antidote being to keep the inmates fully occupied.

From the prisoners point of view these were the harsh realities of prison life in the early nineteenth century. Although few of the general public saw little wrong in all of this, some great social and philosophical figures of the time began to petition for change. Newer prisons, a more humane attitude to the inmates was on the agenda, and Usk prison itself was involved like many others.

Chapter Four
Time and Change

In 1850 the concerns regarding the appointment of John Merrett as Governor of Usk gaol came to a sudden and dramatic conclusion. In February of that year a prisoner identified only as Number 61 attempted to escape by breaking the iron window bars of his cell. However the noise created was overheard by a warder on night duty who quickly foiled the prisoner's bid for freedom. He immediately reported the incident to John Merrett who went at once to the cell in question. He then apparently assaulted prisoner 61 and transferred him handcuffed and half naked to another cell until morning.

This prisoner whilst acknowledging his escape attempt, complained to the Justices about his subsequent treatment at the hands of Merrett. An inquiry into the incident was instigated which resulted in Merrett not only being found guilty of ill treatment but also ordered to forward his resignation. He did so in March 1850 by sending the following letter:

> '*In consequence of the report of the Visiting Magistrates of the House of Correction at Usk, I hereby tender my resignation as Governor and that of my wife as Matron of that prison in three or six months hence, as the Court may request and in doing so I would respectfully name that I have done so on an account of ill health and which has been much impaired by the arduous duties of my office.*'

Although John Merrett's resignation was accepted, he was only given 14 days to leave before the new Governor William Henry Bosworth took up the vacated post. The 1851 Census for the House of Correction showed a total of 73 prisoners, comprising 51 males and 22 females. In his report to the Magistrates Quarter Sessions 18th October 1858, Bosworth summarised the number of committals during the year ending 30th September 1858 as being a total of 770 prisoners, 559 males and 211 females, this included 6 children under 12 years of age. He also included the following note on their education:

Degrees of Instruction	
Neither read nor write	230
Read or write imperfectly	307
Read and write well	21
Superior Instruction	1

A new chaplain had also been appointed at the same time as Bosworth became Governor, the Rev Kenyon Homfray who was a keen supporter of the separate rule. However he was opposed on medical grounds by the surgeon to the gaol Dr James Boulton. By April 1852 Homfray was forced to retire on ill-health grounds to be succeeded by Rev J Cadwallader. The latter wrote about the prisoners in his care in a report to the Magistrates on 14th October 1861:

> '*... their behaviour is generally favourable. Their entire seclusion frequently induces them to entertain serious reflections and religious impressions ... foreign to their former associations. But their abiding genuineness must remain to be evinced in the endurance of future trials ...*'

This advocacy for the separate rule contrasts starkly with the comments of a former prisoner:

> '*Unless one has experienced it, one can have no conception of the effect of close confinement upon the nervous system. People who have not tried it are*

apt to say, 'Well, it's only for twenty-eight days.' But if they were to try what it was like having nothing but white-washed walls to stare at day after day, and neither book nor employment to take one's thoughts, as it were, out of one's self, I don't think they would say anything more about it's being 'only twenty-eight days'"

On 16th October 1871 Dr James Boulton sent in another Medical Report on the prisoners to the Magistrates Assembled Quarter Sessions, the following extract provides an interesting account of the many problems he faced and his response:

'General health pretty good, but through the years we have had a great deal of sickness, so many old and diseased prisoners requiring daily attendance.

Four deaths another over his time, also one under bail, one pardoned on medical grounds, two births, one miscarriage, usual diseases, colds, diarrhoea, venereal delirium, tremors, numerous injuries from fighting. Two cases of Small Pox one a man for trial. An infant one year and eight months died yesterday.

I beg to call your attention to my salary ... the responsibility is very great.'

It will be seen that Boulton was soon to carry out one of the most onerous tasks that a medical man could face. In the Prison Act 1865 the title House of Corrections was replaced by Her Majesty's Prisons, Usk was so renamed and assumed the role of being the major prison in Monmouthshire. However the daily routine of prison life there was soon to be dramatically altered by one, James Henry Gibbs. In 1874 he was found guilty of murder and duly sentenced to death, Usk Prison being nominated as his place of execution. This would be the first hanging within the walls of the prison and a state of unease settled over both staff and prisoners alike. Two warders were selected to be present in the condemned cell with Gibbs up until the morning of the hanging, then they would have to accompany the prisoner together with James Boulton, sundry officials and the hangman to the scaffold to witness the act of execution. A description of the nerve-wracking ordeal they endured with Gibbs is described in Part Three of this book.

Only four years later the infamous Joseph Garcia was convicted at Gloucester Assizes and hanged at Usk for the horrific murders of five members of the Watkins family. The convoluted story of the Llangibby tragedy and the controversy that has dogged it down the ages is retold in detail in Part Two. It still ranks to this day as the worst crime ever committed in this county. As will be seen this was not the last hanging to take place at Usk but only the second of seven!

It was in April 1878 that the Secretary of State announced the formation of Visiting Committees that would report on not only the standards of prisons but also the treatment of the prisoners. A statutory committee was immediately set up for Usk with the then Lord Raglan as a member. The entries in the Minute Books of the new committee frequently state, *'Found the business of the prison going on satisfactorily, saw the prisoners at the wheel and in their worksheds.'* Reading through the minute books the following seem worthy of reproduction:

<u>4th September 1878</u>
A female prisoner complained that her child was suffering from a lack of food. The medical officer asked to attend.

Henry Berry, of Middle Street, was only 14 years old in 1872 when sentenced to 14 days is Usk gaol for stealing £31 in cash. His release from gaol was to followed by three years in a Reform School.

6th January 1879

The attention of the Acting Governor was called to the low temperatures of the cells. 28ºF and 39ºF in the Female Ward in one of which (39) the prisoner was in bed with bad rheumatism.

7th May 1879

Noted that one prisoner had been very violent and that the Acting Governor had placed him in irons.

1st September 1879

Recent floods had broken up part of the brick culvert carrying sewage.

3rd September 1879

Juvenile Benjamin Pritchard will prefer 50 lashes to 4 years at Reformatory.

31st December 1879

The Visiting Magistrates were against the recent practice of prisoners responding in the Chapel services.

Smith's and Carpenter's shops have been erected in the prison.

The Visiting Justices ordered that at executions the Press to be excluded and to admit no one except those whom the Act of Parliament required. They have forwarded this to the High Sheriff for his support of this resolution. He however did not see this in the same light. 'The Committee thinks that sending to the public all the details of the poor wretches dying moments has no tendency to good whatsoever, but is simply pandering to the vitiated taste of a vulgar public.'

21st March 1880

Usk Prison - Annual Staff Salaries

One Governor Everard Milman £200 (plus house, fuel, garden and washing)

Chaplain James Cadwallader £220

Priest Fr. Thomas Croft £25

Warder George Whiting £54 12s

Total Staffing for 1880:

One Governor, One Chaplain, One Priest, One Deputy Governor, Eight Male Warders, One Female Warder, One Engineer, One Gate Porter.

12th January 1881

Prisoners were allowed to earn 'marks' to gain gratuities at a rate of 1d per 10 marks to a maximum of 10/-.

The privilege lately given to prisoners to respond and sing in Chapel works well and is never abused.

Thomas Price was a 27 year old labourer living on Twyn Square. He was sentenced to seven days hard labour in Usk Gaol in March 1873 for the theft of 2oz of tea.

3rd December 1884
Prisoner Charles Lark charged with being in bed at 6.50pm and concealing his oakum (about 1lb in weight) under his bedclothes. Convicted at last Michaelmas of four infringements of prison discipline. A repetition of these offences would probably entail him being flogged.

4 February 1885
Charles Lark again in trouble viz. going to bed with his clothes on at 7.10pm, not completing his task of oakum and throwing the part unfinished at the door of his cell. Sentenced to 6 lashes with cat-o-nine-tails.

5th December 1892
Visited male prisoner Thomas Edwards under sentence of Death. The prisoner asked permission to write to certain relations and friends of whom the Chief Warder in charge has a list, and I gave him necessary permission for this purpose.

It can be readily seen by the above that the Visiting Committee although aware of the realities of prison life were also a benign and caring authority. When they interviewed prisoners in their cells no warders were allowed to be present enabling them to discuss any problems they were experiencing. There is no doubt that the Government's initiative in this area produced a welcome improvement in prison conditions and in the treatment of the prisoners themselves.

Visiting Statutory Committee at Usk Gaol in the 1880s.

The *'Records of Prisoners'* book for Usk covering the years 1911-1912 makes fascinating reading where the sentences handed down for the various crimes still have the ability to shock. From the hundreds of entries in the book I have selected a small sample to illustrate this, although some I must admit tend to bring a wry smile to the face! Most of the male prisoners had their occupations merely listed as labourers, together with colliers and seamen, whilst the females were frequently described as maids or prostitutes.

Their activities range from the more obvious ones such as stealing and drunkeness to crimes such as 'sleeping out', 'desertion' and 'begging'. The sentences were often short usually up to three months, with or without hard labour. Those receiving longer sentences were usually sent on to Dartmoor for completion. A bleak prospect no doubt!

Selected Prisoners and Sentences 1911-1912

Date	Name	Age	Occupation	Offence	Sentence
1911	Richard Cooper	39	Labourer	Stole overcoat (Persistent)	3yrs h/l
	George Pegler	54	Gardener	Stole pair brass candlesticks	3yrs
	Daniel Edmunds	32	Collier	Salmon poaching	1m
	Arthur Davies	55	Schoolmaster	Stealing money	6m h/l
	Samuel Litson	21	Labourer	Incest with sister	3yrs h/l
	Henry Gibson	18	Labourer	Stealing coins & false teeth	6wks h/l
	Archibald Fox	19	Hotel Boots	Stealing bicycle	Borstal
	Olaf Hansen	21	Sailor	Stealing mouth organ	7 days
1912	Rose Kennard	28	Parlour Maid	Stealing lace & umbrella	3m h/l
	Edgar Warman	36	Labourer	Stealing 3 ducks	21 days h/l
	William Jillson	33	Collier	Underage sex with girl	10yrs
	Francis Simmons	23	Actor	Shooting at police	6yrs h/l
	Will Wiltshire	38	Ragsman	Blowing horn in street	7 days
	Samuel Bartlett	35	Labourer	Stealing one plaice	1m
	Sam Winkworth	37	Barman	Forged postal order	3yrs
	Albert Williams	23	Labourer	Stealing 8 dead rabbits	14 days

Besides the infamous Garcia case, perhaps the prison's most 'celebrated guest' was Margaret Haig Thomas. The only daughter of a wealthy Monmouthshire man she was educated at Notting Hill High School before gaining a degree at Somerville College Oxford. After marrying a neighbour Sir Humphrey Mackworth, her and her father were returning from a visit to America on board the 'S.S. Lusitania' when it was sunk by a torpedo from a German submarine on 7th May 1915; by a miracle both survived. Her marriage however was not a happy one, he was

Margaret Haig Thomas Viscountess Rhondda.

The New York Times. EXTRA 8:30 A.M.

LUSITANIA SUNK BY A SUBMARINE, PROBABLY 1,260 DEAD; TWICE TORPEDOED OFF IRISH COAST; SINKS IN 15 MINUTES; CAPT. TURNER SAVED, FROHMAN AND VANDERBILT MISSING; WASHINGTON BELIEVES THAT A GRAVE CRISIS IS AT HAND

essentially a 'hunting & shooting' man whilst Margaret Mackworth was a more reflective yet strong-willed person.

SS Lusitania.

To his great consternation her imagination had become caught by the drama of Emiline Pankhurst and the Suffragette Movement, her inherent feminism coming to the fore. She further antagonised him by inviting Mrs Pankhurst to speak at Newport. In the event she sent her daughter Sylvia, but a later invitation to stay with Lady Mackworth was firmly vetoed by her husband! On 15th July 1913 Margaret Mackworth was charged and convicted of placing a bomb in a letterbox at Newport and at the subsequent court hearing Lady Mackworth was given the option of either paying a fine or going to prison for one month. Being a true believer in the women's movement she chose imprisonment at Usk. As a suffragette she was allowed to wear her own clothes rather than the prison garments but this was her only privilege. It must have been a traumatic moment for a lady of gentle breeding when the door of her cell was bolted for the first time.

The prison records show that on the same day two other women Elizabeth Welsh and Eleanor Parr also began their sentences at Usk, both having been convicted of using obscene language and indulging in prostitution. Lady Margaret Mackworth, Viscountess Rhondda had come face to face with the realities of the poor and the wretched, where paying a fine was no alternative to imprisonment. In one way it was what she and other feminists were fighting for, although I suspect it would have made little sense to the other two women.

Her determination was shown when she refused all food and only took water at mealtimes. This proved too much for her husband and within six days he had paid the fine of £20 4s 6d and had her released. It is not known whether she approved of this action by Sir Humphrey but no doubt the conditions she encountered during her short stay gave her plenty of food for thought. Whilst she was perhaps the most famous prisoner to reside at Usk, there were other characters when reading through the records that stamped an indelible mark on the history of the prison.

Patrick Ryan was, using current jargon, a serial offender though of the more minor types of criminal activity. In reality his story is one of a life blighted by anger and frustration yet there is an aura of sadness at the end of it. He incurred well over seventy convictions between 1889 and 1915, having spent most of his adult life in prison interspersed with brief spells of freedom. Many affrays with the police were due to his boisterous Irish nature no doubt enhanced by heavy drinking. He was listed as a labourer living in and around Newport with his equally raucous friends. As the years passed his offences became more and more mundane descending eventually into begging and indecent behaviour.

He could be described as a 'broth of a boy' but he lived in an age when desperate poverty was the accepted lot of a vast majority of the population. His story throws a melancholic light on a period when a strapping lad from Ireland with shining eyes and a merry laugh somehow reserved it for the hollow echoes of Usk prison. Men of his generation either died in wretchedness or fell victims to the whims of Generals on the Western Front.

It was of course foreseen that during the First World War crime levels would decrease simply because most able-bodied men (and indeed youths!) were in France fighting for their country. However a crime new to the statute book, that of being termed an 'alien', became a common theme with many of Austrian and German origins, that is non-British, being interned. Again we see prisoners arriving at Usk from military backgrounds on charges such as 'Desertion', 'Disobeying a lawful command', or 'Absent without leave.' Despite these intakes the population of Usk prison rapidly decreased.

Thirty years old Mabel Dale acquired some kind fame in that she was the last female to be imprisoned there after being convicted on a charge of prostitution. She in fact joined four other women all of whom were transferred on 3rd April 1918 to the prison in Cardiff. A source of more inmates came from a totally different direction. The 'troubles' in Ireland had flared and twenty Sinn Fein activists were brought to Usk to serve their sentences. One sad epitaph was gained by one of these men, a Richard Coleman, who was never to see his homeland again as he passed away within the prison walls on 9th December 1918.

Within four years the prison was closed and remained so for another seventeen years. Our story has neared its end for in 1939 it was transformed into a Closed Borstal and operated as such until 1964. It now served as a Detention Centre until in 1983 when it changed yet again now acting as a Youth Custody Centre. In May 1990 it became an Adult Category C prison dealing with those convicted of sexual offences.

The prison system and outlook today radically differs from its Victorian counterpart. There is a Comber Unit designed to accommodate older prisoners, whilst cells now have televisions incorporated in them, there being capacity for 242 prisoners. There is also available drug counselling, card phones and personal officer schemes. I wonder what Lady Mackworth or Patrick Ryan would have made of it!

The harshness of Victorian Sentencing.

PART TWO

Joseph Garcia and the Llangibby Murders

*   *   *

Chapter Five
'From little acorns...'

It has to be admitted that the year 1878 was not a particularly auspicious one. Queen Victoria was on the throne and still in mourning for her beloved Prince Albert who had succumbed to typhoid fever some 17 years before.

At Abercarn there occurred one of the worst pit disasters ever when a fire from escaping methane gas took 268 lives with a further 82 badly burned. Nearby Blaenavon achieved a certain degree of fame by perfecting the Bessemer process for producing fine steel. Yet in the history of crime in the county of Monmouthshire,

Sidney Gilchrist Thomas who with his cousin Percy Gilchrist perfected the Bessemer process.

The Vale of Usk.

this year of 1878 was to witness one of the most appalling and brutal acts of murder on record, in fact multiple murders. A family of five were literally slaughtered in their home, a home nestling in the most quiet and beautiful part of the countryside that lies between Usk and Caerleon, near the village of Llangibby. This is the story of their murders, with the subsequent arrest, conviction and execution of the guilty person.

Of course myths and legends have always swirled around the towns and villages of Wales, each generation passing them on to the next. Over the years many become transmuted into absolute facts. However in this case there is a mystery - 130 years after the events of that dreadful day a query still exists as to whether Joseph Garcia, the man who eventually went to the gallows actually committed the crime. The evidence against him, although entirely circumstantial was truly overwhelming, yet as we shall see a mystery still remains.

The summer of the year 1878 to the delight of the British public had been consistently hot, with the sun pouring down day after day from a clear blue sky. It was on one such bright July morning that Joseph Garcia finally stepped out of the dank shadows of the cells of Usk gaol, a free man. Little is known of his early life. What can be gleaned is that he was born in 1857 at the small town of Puebla in the province of Valencia. Garcia in fact came from a middle class and highly respected farming family whose household consisted of his father and mother, three brothers and a single daughter.

He was by all accounts an indolent youth who at a very early age decided to enlist in the Republican Army which was then at war with the pretender to the Spanish throne, Don Carlos. This war between the Carlists and Republicans was a particularly brutal affair, with many acts of violence and cruelty, atrocities being almost commonplace. It was later suggested in a local newspaper, The Usk Gleaner, that Garcia's experiences in this war had led him to having a low estimate of human life and thus capable of cold blooded murder. This is a notoriously unsafe proposition as millions have fought in innumerable wars over the centuries, yet on returning to their homelands have not adopted the guise of homicidal maniacs.

Garcia was an itinerant Spanish seaman who arrived in Newport sometime during 1877. It was on the 27th September of that year that he broke into the home of David Williams and his wife who resided in the parish of St Brides, Wentloog. It was reported that Mrs Williams disturbed Garcia whilst he was searching the house although she initially thought that it was her son. However on realising her mistake she found herself being threatened by a stranger who, according to her, was brandishing a knife. He quickly absconded from the place leaving her unharmed but was soon arrested by Sergeant McGrath of the local police. He was duly convicted on 16th October at the quarter sessions at Usk of the offence of burglary and sentenced to nine months hard labour in the local gaol.

His presence in Wales can most likely be attributed to the search abroad for sources of iron for the foundries of the valleys. Local seams were becoming exhausted and fresh supplies had been located in the Basque region of Spain. Thus the areas around the seaports in Cardiff and Newport soon became home to a multiracial society, with some of the Spaniards eventually deciding to stay and make their homes here. The Bute area was a recognised centre for such mixed populations. It can

Alexandra Dock, Newport.

be surmised that Garcia was one of those who roamed Cardiff and the surrounding district finally arriving in nearby Newport. Little did he know that when he was freed on that July morning he would never again see his homeland or family.

He was released with a number of other prisoners at 8am on Tuesday 16th July 1878 by warder George Whiting. The regulations allowed prisoners the return of their possessions and the issue of a rail ticket. Garcia's included a jacket, trousers, blue cap, a pair of canvas shoes and an additional set of Blucher boots. In addition he also had a white handkerchief within which were wrapped a white cotton shirt, two neckerchiefs, a flannel smock and a purse holding some English and Spanish coins. The rail ticket would have been purchased by the warder, who in turn would be financed by the Discharged Prisoners' Aid Society. The local gentry supported this Society by subscription, although it could be interpreted as slightly ingenuous, for if the released prisoners took advantage of their generosity they were unlikely to remain in the Usk area, thus avoiding any future problems.

Whiting patiently tried to explain this offer of a rail ticket to Garcia, who spoke very little English, but eventually the Spaniard managed to indicate that he would rather go to Newport than the warder's suggestion of Cardiff. Whiting momentarily left Garcia with the other released prisoners in order to bring out a female inmate who was also being freed that morning. Returning a few moments later he found that Garcia had disappeared. Whiting did not realise it at the time, but the train of events at Garcia's release would itself become the subject of a later inquiry. This was because there existed a warder's trick of releasing discharged prisoners and conveniently pocketing their rail money. This deeply upset George Whiting, as he was known as a man of integrity who never indulged in such practices. This did nothing to deter village gossip and rumour, which also inferred that if the staff at the gaol had been more alert then perhaps the horrific events that were to follow could have been avoided. Whiting himself was a local man living with his wife and children at

14 New Market Street, Usk. Home in 1878 of George Whiting warder at Usk who released Garcia from prison.

14 New Market Street which borders the River Usk. He must have felt keenly these unfair insinuations as he carried on his daily life in the village. In fact it was he who gave an excellent report on Garcia's time at the prison, describing him as a 'model' prisoner, who caused no problems either with warders or other inmates during his confinement. Garcia would have perhaps been even more isolated than the others due to his lack of English. This report does add to the mystery of the Spaniard's subsequent behaviour.

Eastern Monmouthshire is essentially farming country, the Vale of Usk lying in a broad sweep beneath the heights of Wentwood. In the late Victorian era Caerleon, Llangibby, Usk and Raglan resembled beads on a necklace, strung out as they were between Newport in the south and the town of Abergavenny in the north. Dotted on the hillsides around these villages were numerous whitewashed farmhouses glinting in the summer suns. Usk was then home to about 1,500 souls, whilst the nearby hamlet of Llangibby held a mere 500 or so. In that idyllic summer of 1878 they dozed and slumbered, secure in their isolation, for the only means of transport besides walking, was the horse. Everyone knew everyone else, and often were related through marriage, so that any visitor would almost certainly be noticed, those from foreign lands being virtually unknown. The Caerleon-born author, Arthur Machen was to write in his book The Chronicle of Clemendy (1888) the following evocative description:

> '... if you once cross the bridge and get into Uske, you will have plenty to look at without thinking of Wentwood, that is, if you are fond of quaint houses, wild old-fashioned gardens and odd nooks and corners of every sort. And, better than all, there are old tales and legends still lingering about the

Arthur Machen (1863-1947)

sunny streets, and sleeping on the settles next to the fire; but it is getting rather difficult to wake them up now, because you see they are very old.'

In Victorian days the village of Llangibby (named after St Cybi), was tiny and compact, and as with other such hamlets, it was structured around the Church, the School and the Inn. The church was founded in the sixth century by St Cybi, a distant relative of the more famous St David. He hailed from Cornwall and travelled throughout Wales in the company of a number of monks, eventually reaching Monmouthshire. After crossing the River Usk, they set up their tents in a meadow bordering a small village.

The entire area was ruled by a pagan, King Etholric, who became incensed by the presence of the wanderers on his land. One morning he rode out with his men, determined to either move or kill the intruders, but on arriving at the campsite and confronting St Cybi he was suddenly struck blind. In great fear and despair he pleaded with St Cybi to help him regain his sight. This the saint accomplished so making the pagan a believer. Legend holds that Cybi's stone in the meadow by Llangibby marks the exact spot where this miracle took place.

A second legend has it that the devil entered Wentwood heights and looked down on Llangibby where he spied the great stone. He desired to take this land for himself, in order to do so he threw quoits in an attempt to place one around the stone. They all fell short of their target so the elements of Envy and Malice have never managed to gain a foothold in Llangibby!

Cybi's Stone.

'The Stone of Cybi stands for all to see,
In meadow green below Llangibby.'

William Watkins was not a Monmouthshire man, but was born at Whitchurch near Hereford where he spent most of his early years. His father, of the same Christian name, had been widowed, his first wife bearing him seven children, one of whom was William. When his father married for the second time William further acquired four stepbrothers and sisters. Families in those days were frequently large in number, as offspring were needed to maintain the family income, usually by labouring on the land. It was some years later that William migrated to Monmouthshire, being employed at various times at Llandowlas, Hendrew, Rhyadr, Estavarney and other farms in the area. Although he had a reputation of being a good worker he rarely stayed long at any particular farm. It was while he was employed in Mr Crump's service at Estavarney, that William began courting a young woman named Elizabeth Ann Jasper, a servant in the employment of Mr Gething of Penrose. She had already borne an illegitimate son, whether William was the father is not known, but on her wedding day in August 1862 at Caerleon church, she was again pregnant. It is recorded that William was aged 21 and his wife a year older; their child, Mary Ann was born two months later.

Over the next few years Elizabeth was to raise five more children, Catherine, Arthur, Charlotte, Alice and Frederick. Although they had a large family, they didn't remain in one place for too long, constantly criss-crossing the Vale of

The cottage at Llangibby in which William Watkins and his family lived.

Usk, living in a variety of dwellings from farmhouses to small cottages. It is very likely that having to walk to work each day, left William no option but to change places so as to be near his workplace. Eventually by 1878 they had settled in a simple, rather bleak looking cottage situated in its own garden on the outskirts of Llangibby village, a little distance from the nearest dwelling. They were already known to the local people, as some years earlier they had been living at Rock Cottage just north of the village, but Elizabeth had not been happy there, and it was through an arrangement with Mr John Morgan of Cefn Llech farm that they managed to move to the house on the turnpike-road.

Like many men of his station, William was forced to turn his hand to a wide variety of tasks in order to sustain his wife and large family. Indeed they began to prosper in a small way due to the success that Elizabeth made with the selling of produce from their garden. Her husband had at one time worked for Warren Evans, a waggoner in the village, but by early 1878 he had found employment with Jeremiah Church, the owner of a large holding, Cwm Farm, which lay to the north-west of Llangibby. As mid-summer approached, only three of their children were still at home, the other four were in service locally. On the morning of Tuesday 16th July, some hours before the release of Garcia from Usk prison, William together with a young lad named Frank James had set out for Cwm Farm to pull swedes. William eventually returned home late that evening, to find his three children, Charlotte (aged 8), Alice (aged 5) and Frederick (aged 4) asleep in their upstairs bedroom. It was around 10 o'clock that same night that a Miss Ann James passed by, and noticed that the house door was open. About forty minutes later she made her return journey and this time observed that the door was now shut, but there was a light in the bedroom. The following morning it was recorded that a meal of bacon, potatoes and beans was still on the kitchen table. They were never to finish that meal, nor were they or the sleeping children ever to see the light of dawn of the next day.

Chapter Six
'It is always the impossible that happens...'

Throughout the hours of darkness an eerie silence drifted from room to room in the house of the Watkins family, for the normal sounds of breathing of incumbent sleepers no longer disturbed the quiet. As first light appeared the full horror of the events of the previous evening would be laid bare for all to see.

On that Wednesday morning, a little before seven o'clock, Frank James, only eleven years of age, had finished his breakfast, and with a goodbye to his mother set off down the dusty road towards that fateful house. He lived at Cefn Llech cottage with his parents, two brothers and a sister, his home being less than half a mile away from the Watkins' place. Has had been the case throughout the month, the early morning was slightly cool before the full rising of the sun, but the clear skies indicated that another hot day could be expected. Young Frank approached the wooden gate of the Watkins' garden; with perhaps his mind on other things he unconsciously lifted the latch and pushed it open. His lone echoing footsteps now came to a sudden halt, as his widening eyes saw a totally unexpected sight. Fear spread a deathly pallor over his normally ruddy complexion, for there lying full-length on the path in a pool of congealed blood was the still body of Elizabeth Watkins.

MURDER OF FIVE PERSONS Nr NEWPORT-MONMOUTHSHE

DISCOVERING THE BODIES.

Momentarily paralysed with fright, Frank was suddenly galvanised and with a scream he fled crying along the road, back to the safety of his home, where the terrified boy managed between sobs to blurt out his story to Mary his mother. In the meantime 22 year old John Evans riding on horseback from Coed Y Fon farm near Tredunnock was on his way to the Smithy at Llangibby to have his mowing machine repaired. His journey also took him past the Watkins house. Being on horseback enabled him to see immediately not only the body of Elizabeth Watkins on the path, but also to his horror that of her husband lying at an angle to her. William was similarly on his back, with the macabre difference of having Sweet William flowers that had been torn from the garden, sprinkled

Standing at the back of this family portrait is John Evans of Coed y Fon farm, who on the morning of 17th July 1878 discovered the bodies of William and Elizabeth Watkins.

over his upturned face. They were both literally awash with blood.

Seeing that both were dead, he rode frantically to Cefn Llech farm to raise the alarm, whereupon John Morgan accompanied him back to the house. After a quick examination of the bodies of William and Elizabeth, Morgan went up to the front door and pushed it inwards. Almost immediately he was enveloped in clouds of thick black smoke that billowed down the staircase, filling the rooms below. He and John Evans attempted to see if they could catch sight of the three children, but were beaten back by the intensity of the acrid fumes. Morgan then fetched water but was unsuccessful in trying to put out the fire.

It was now approaching 8 o'clock, and the shocking events at the Watkins house was beginning to seep around the immediate neighbourhood. Llangibby in those days could boast two inns, directly opposite each other. On one side was 'The White Hart', still in business to this day, whilst on the other was 'The Fox and Hounds' whose innkeeper at the time was Thomas Day. On hearing the news he departed on horseback, covering the half-mile in a matter of minutes. On arrival, being made aware of the problem with the smoke, he managed to prise open a side window in order to release the fumes. He then noticed a ladder in the outhouse, and placing it against the wall of the house managed to crawl on to the roof. Once there he tore furiously at the tiles and plaster to eventually create a sizeable hole, allowing the exit of the smoke. Once more on the ground, he re-entered the house and bravely fought his way up the stairs.

On flinging open the bedroom door, the sight that met his eyes resembled a vision from the nethermost bowels of hell, for a sickening odour of burnt flesh assailed his nostrils as he entered the room.

The floor of the children's bedroom had burned completely through to the living room below, whilst feathers from the bed and pillows were badly scorched. One child was lying with her head between a storage box and the bedstead. Another was partly lying under the bed face downwards, whilst a third was in an inner recess. All three had been savagely attacked with a knife, one being also badly burned. The eldest child, Charlotte, who had stab wounds to her back, had attempted to reach the window to call for help. The wounds on these poor children far exceeded in severity even those inflicted on their parents. Thomas Day pulled the two bodies on the bed to the floor as the mattress and pillows were still smouldering.

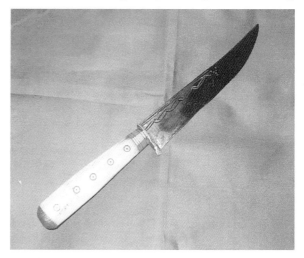

The knife believed to be the weapon used to murder the five members of the Watkins family in the summer of 1878.

In the kitchen, two half empty teacups were found on the table, and some slices of cold bacon were still in the frying pan. The house appeared to have been ransacked; broken furniture was scattered everywhere as if a violent struggle had taken place.

Meanwhile news had reached Caerleon police station and Sergeant Povall rode immediately towards Llangibby, arriving at the cottage at about 9.30am. On receiving similar information, Sergeant Rowan of Usk police had commandeered a horse and he joined Povall at the grim scene, both making detailed notes of their observations. It must have caused deep shock to both officers, as their normal duties would have included investigations of poaching, thieving, drunkenness, abuse and other comparatively minor misdemeanours. Neither had ever experienced anything like this, and would never again in their careers.

By midday, the officials at Usk gaol had issued the following description of a possible suspect for the murders:

'Yusaf, alias Joseph Garcia, a Spanish sailor age 21, 5ft 5 in high, proportionate figure, dark complexion, black hair, dark eyes, dressed in a blue blouse.'

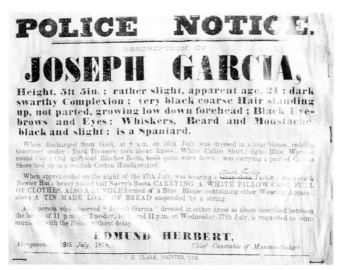

Police Notice issued for the arrest of Joseph Garcia.

At this distance in time, the message that he could be a possible suspect seems rather strange in that Garcia not only received an exemplary report from warder George Whiting following his period of imprisonment, but also was released along with a number of other prisoners. Why should Garcia be more culpable than any of the others?

Using the telegraph, this information was circulated that day to Newport and Cardiff police stations. All available police officers were put on full alert, instructed to keep a lookout particularly at railway stations, for a person answering to that description.

As Garcia had now been designated the main suspect based on the prison authorities announcement, it is worth attempting to trace his movements after leaving the gaol the morning before. There were a number of sightings of the Spaniard on the Tuesday, although as is usual in such cases, some of them could be deemed extremely doubtful. Tramps in the countryside were then a common sight, and their naturally dishevelled appearance coupled with begrimed faces and hands could easily be misconstrued to be those of a person of foreign origin. The prison at Usk lies at the distal end of Maryport Street, next to the Sessions House, so on leaving the building there are two routes that may be taken to Newport. Turning immediately left would take you on the old road, passing through Llanlowell and Kemys Inferior to eventually arrive at Caerleon via Bulmore. The other would lead you through the town, over the river bridge and left at the T-junction when you would pass through Llanbadoc, Llangibby to again finally reach Caerleon. By the following accounts it is obvious that Garcia took the latter route.

A positive sighting of Garcia was made by Harriet Bowyer, a resident of Llanbadoc, who when travelling towards Caerleon noticed a person resembling the description of Garcia lying near a stile apparently asleep. The time was around eleven o'clock on the Tuesday morning, and was within a hundred yards of the Watkins' cottage. Miss Bowyer returned later that afternoon at about 4pm and noticed the same man again asleep in a nearby field.

A second sighting was made by a Mrs Ann Gwatkin who lived at Llangibby and claimed to have answered the door to Garcia at about seven o'clock in the evening of the same day. She gave him a drink of water, and he managed to ask in broken English the way to Newport. Mrs Gwatkin pointed out the road and the direction he should take, which in fact would lead him past the Watkins' cottage. She never saw him again. An odd report came from a Mr Humphries, post cart driver who was journeying on the Tuesday evening between Abergavenny and Usk. At Llanellen, which lies due north of Usk, he claimed that he was approached by the suspect who begged him for a lift to Newport. The driver refused to do this as he didn't like the disreputable appearance of the man. Given the evidence of both Harriet Bowyer and Ann Gwatkin, the only conclusion that can be made is that the cart driver was mistaken, and that it was probably a tramp that he had spoken with.

Nothing more was heard or seen of Garcia that Tuesday and this disappearance from view stretched through most of the next day, when the bodies had been discovered. It was nearly midnight on the Wednesday when he finally appeared in Marshes Road on the outskirts of Newport, carrying a large bundle. This road has long since disappeared, but at the time lay to the west of the town. He was observed by PC Tooze of Newport police, who compared the description he had been given of Garcia, against the man standing in front of him. He decided that this nightwalker was not the suspect and Garcia was allowed to continue on his way.

A short while later the Spaniard was in Mill Street where he met a Newport decorator of Swedish extraction by the name of Albert Yhnell. He asked the tradesman the way to the railway station as he wished to go to Cardiff, whereupon Yhnell kindly escorted him the rest of the way. John Jones, the night foreman of the Great Western Railway at Newport, answered the knocking at the door by Yhnell, who enquired if he would admit a sailor who was bound for Cardiff. Jones informed him that the next train to Cardiff wasn't due until 2.30am. Yhnell then left as Garcia asked Jones for a drink of water, the foreman pointing to a drinking fountain outside of the station entrance.

THE ARREST

Whilst he was at the fountain, PC Tooze appeared once more, and this time asked him what country he was from. Garcia replied, 'Portugee.' Tooze now decided that he would go and speak with Sergeant McGrath whom he knew had known Garcia from his arrest for housebreaking the previous year.

The arrest of Garcia.

When McGrath finally arrived, he immediately recognised the man resting on the station bench as being Joseph Garcia, and promptly arrested him.

Later the Watch Committee, who administrated the police force in those days, met to discuss the events surrounding the apprehension of Garcia. After much reflection they decided that PC Tooze had been in dereliction of his duty in not arresting Garcia immediately, as they pointed out that the prisoner could so easily have taken fright and escaped. A result of their deliberations, PC Tooze was given a reprimand and a penalty deduction was made against his wages for that week.

Chapter Seven

'From the promise to the deed is a day's journey...'

By now rumour had fed upon rumour, so that the entire county was in a high state of ferment over the killings. Of course the murder of children always produces a profound response in society, when overwhelming anger fuels a need to exact revenge upon the would-be perpetrators. It was also inevitable that the facts as known to the police would be garbled and twisted by the time they entered the public domain. In Llangibby and its environs, the shocking events would have engendered a state of fear, so that as night approached, doors and windows of the many isolated dwellings would be firmly shut and secured. It must have come as a great relief to this small community when news of an arrest finally reached their ears.

Garcia was taken in handcuffs to the county police cell, which in those days was rather incongruously sited beneath the Victoria Hall Theatre in Bridge Street. Eighteen years later a fire largely destroyed the playhouse, whereupon it was replaced by the Lyceum Theatre. This survived until 1960, when it was demolished to make way for a line of shops. Today the site is occupied by a modern cinema and wine bar. To gain evidence with regard to Garcia's movements, the police issued the following public notice which was displayed at various points throughout east Gwent:

The Lyceum Theatre.

POLICE NOTICE

JOSEPH GARCIA

Height 5ft. 5in.; rather slightly built, apparent age, 21; dark swarthy Complexion; very black coarse Hair standing up, not parted, growing low down forehead; Black Eye-brows and Eyes; Whiskers, Beard and Moustache, black and slight; is a Spaniard.

When discharged from Gaol, at 8am on 16th July, was dressed in a blue blouse, reddish Guernsey under; Dark Trousers torn about knees; White Calico Shirt; light Blue Worsted Round Cap; Old worn-out Blucher Boots, heels quite worn down; was carrying a pair of Canvas Shoes tied up in a reddish Cotton Handkerchief.

When apprehended on the night of the 17th July, was wearing a dark tweed Jacket; hard black Bowler Hat; heavy nailed half Navvy's Boots, CARRYING A WHITE PILLOW CASE FULL OF CLOTHES, ALSO A BUNDLE formed of a Blue Blouse containing other Wearing Apparel, also a TIN MADE LOAF OF BREAD suspended by a string.

Any person who observed 'Joseph Garcia' dressed in either dress as above described between the hours of 11pm on Tuesday, 16th, on Wednesday, 17th July is requested to communicate with the Police without delay.

Edmund Herbert *Chief Constable of Monmouthshire*

It was soon realised by the local police that their prisoner didn't understand enough English to be able to answer their questions. Subsequently a request was made for an interpreter, the clerk to the Spanish Consul taking that role. Garcia was then informed of the serious charges that were to be made against him. He calmly protested his innocence. The police in the meantime had not only searched him, but had minutely examined the bundle he had with him when arrested. This proved to be highly incriminating, for not only did he appear to be wearing the shoes of William Watkins, but also a double pair of trousers, one of which again might well have belonged to the dead man. The bundle also realised a number of items from the Watkins' household, including clothes and a small loaf of bread. To these charges Garcia explained through the interpreter that he had simply found them.

By the following morning, Thursday 18th July, a large crowd had gathered outside the police station in Bridge Street. As the day wore on they became more and more vociferous, fuelled no doubt by the excessive consumption of alcohol. The police were becoming increasingly uneasy at the ugliness of a crowd that began to acquire the hallmarks of a lynch mob. It is odd to reflect that we usually perceive these happenings as belonging to the old Wild West where phrases such as string 'em up, or hang 'em high came into our consciousness through the medium of 'Cowboy and Indian' films.

Yet even today elements of this sort of behaviour still exist, although it is usually well controlled by the police. It can be seen when police vans are transporting prisoners to the law courts for trial. People line the entrance yelling abuse or hurling missiles at the passing vans. It's only really a matter of degree that separates this behaviour from the past.

Their anxieties over an increasingly hostile crowd outside were relieved by the notification that a special sessions under the chairmanship of John James was to be held that day at Caerleon. At 1.30 on Thursday 18th July, the prisoner under heavy escort was taken from Newport to Caerleon police station in a horse-drawn cab. At the beginning of their journey they were pursued by a howling mob, baying for Garcia's blood, but gradually the speed of the horses left them far behind. Of course this show of violent emotions, although here in extreme, reflected the general mood of the people of Monmouthshire after the details of the killings became known. The phrase too good to hang comes to mind!

When Garcia finally arrived at Caerleon police station, he was taken immediately to be examined before the magistrates and attending officers. Another vociferous crowd outside of the station gave full vent to their feelings as the prisoner was brought out. The police court was itself overflowing with as many as possible wanting to catch their first glimpse of Garcia; others even climbed on adjoining buildings and walls to peer hopefully through the windows of the building.

Those officiating comprised of the magistrate, Mr John James, Major Herbert the Chief Constable, Mr Hopton Williams, Mr T E Cooke, and Superintendent Mackintosh. Sergeant Povall brought in the charge sheet. There was a certain amount of subdued talk, whisperings, as if all were waiting for a church service to begin. Then silence descended as a police officer brought in the accused, when every pair of eyes swivelled and strained in one direction. What did a murderer look like? Could you tell from his appearance the evilness of his nature? No doubt many other questions flitted through the minds of those present in the room that hot day in July, as they craned forward to obtain a better view.

What they saw was a man wearing a blue blouse, sometimes referred to as a monkey jacket, full buttoned up to the neck. He proved to be a slightly built man, with thin features, a nose which in profile was long and sharp, an oval face of olive complexion surmounted by a shock of thick, black curly hair. He had small darting eyes, was seen to be clean-shaven, and behaved in a quiet, composed manner.

The clerk to the magistrates read out to the waiting court the charge, that Joseph Garcia had committed the wilful murder of William, Elizabeth, Charlotte, Alice and Frederick Watkins at Llangibby in this county, on the 17th July. He then asked, 'Do you wish to say anything why you should not be remanded. You understand what I tell you?'

The prisoner murmured, 'Italian, Italian.'

The clerk replied, 'No, it is English; do you understand?'

Major Herbert then interrupted, 'He does not understand Italian; the Spanish Consul's clerk attended, and interpreted the charge to him in my hearing this morning, and he said he did not do it. The Consul's clerk asked him how he accounted for the property in his possession, which belonged, or which we imagined to belong, to the murdered people, and he said he found it. I think Sir, that if you will take that statement from me, although it is not strictly evidence, it would, perhaps be sufficient for a remand. As the man was only apprehended this morning, we are not prepared today to go fully into the case, and perhaps you will take it from me, and grant a short remand upon that.'

The major also pointed out that the accused was seen in the vicinity of the house, so that a remand for two or three days would seem reasonable, and allow them to make a full case. Mr James agreed to remand Garcia until Monday, and enquired of the major if he thought that Garcia understood. The Chief Constable then endeavoured to speak to Garcia in Italian, but he only shook his head. Major Herbert added that it would be necessary to inform the Spanish Consul, as he had expressed a wish to attend personally, with an interpreter being present on the Monday. The major finally directed the magistrate's attention to scratches on Garcia's left cheek, just below the eye. He pointed out that as there was no medical person present at the hearing, he couldn't say what had caused them, it could have been a knife, fingernails, or even brambles. The prisoner was then led back to his cell.

The next day, Friday 19th July, saw the inquest, conducted by the coroner, Mr W.H. Brewer into the deaths of the five members of the Watkins family. The White Hart Inn at Llangibby was chosen as the venue, where twelve male

The White Hart Inn, Llangibby.

jurors were asked to assemble. It must here be acknowledged that in a number of ways, what was judicially acceptable in Victorian times would be viewed as inadmissible today. Mr Brewer's opening remarks to the jury were highly prejudicial to the accused, in addition to the fact that the local newspapers had, with bold headlines, already branded Garcia as the murderer.

Firstly Brewer rightly commented on the appalling nature of the crime, and then added, 'Of course, gentlemen, so far as we are able to judge, the man is in custody that committed this act. Of course we can't tell that as yet, but I still believe so.' So much for the unassailable right of every person to be regarded as innocent until proven guilty! The coroner's remarks were naturally reported in the newspapers, so that any potential juror for the forthcoming trial at the assizes would more than likely to be so influenced.

By mid-morning the jurors, with their foreman Hopton Williams, had left The White Hart Inn and were slowly making their way to the Watkins' cottage to inspect the bodies of the five victims. I don't suppose that any of them particularly relished this task, as even the sight of one corpse may be regarded as an onerous duty. Here, two adults and three children had lain for all of two days in the July heat, exhibiting not only the most savage injuries imaginable, but also had been already subjected to a post mortem. It must have certainly affected the twelve men as they gazed in undisguised horror at the mutilated corpses.

Badly shaken, they eventually returned to the inn where they listened to the evidence

Dr. James Boulton.
Medical Practitioner and Surgeon of Usk.

of a number of witnesses. Of course no one had actually been present at the murders, but it was important to try to establish the movements of Garcia after his release from Usk prison. The police officers gave details of his arrest and the contents of the bundle in his possession. Also present was Dr James Boulton, the medical practitioner and surgeon who was asked to relay his post mortem findings. Besides holding surgery at 29 New Market Street for the people of Usk, he also had taken up the position of surgeon to the local House of Correction. Six years later his son, Donald took over from him.

At the conclusion of Dr Boulton's evidence, the coroner summed up all aspects of the case for the jury. By his words it is obvious that he had already assigned guilt to Garcia, 'I can see no doubt in this matter .... from what you have seen .... the prisoner must leave you but very little doubt that he is the party who did it.

I think that you would come to that conclusion among yourselves.' This is not just clarifying the facts for the jurors, but directing them as well! It will come as no surprise that they took less then five minutes to reach a verdict of wilful murder against Joseph Garcia.

The jurors, perhaps still in shock over the dreadful sight of the bodies, expressed their sorrow over the tragedy by agreeing to donate the jury fees to the burial fund. At six in the evening of that same day, a sad cortege bearing the coffins of the dead members of the Watkins family slowly threaded its way to the awaiting grave in the cemetery surrounding the Church of St Cybi in Llangibby. Concerns were voiced by some of the local people that the funeral was too precipitate, that many of the friends and family of the deceased were unable to attend. However I suspect that consideration was given to the unquestioned deterioration of the corpses since the killings, and prudence would have indicated rapid interment. The service had been conducted by Rev Ffolliott Lynch Salisbury, the sudden taking of five lives adding a profound degree of sombreness to the proceedings. The coffins of the father and mother being placed first in the grave, followed by those of the children.

Grave of Watkins family at Llangibby.

St Cibi's Church, Llangibby.

45

Chapter Eight
'Law and justice are not always the same thing...'

Science declares that for every action there is a reaction, unfortunately the same rule can also be assigned to human behaviour. I say unfortunately because the response to crimes can vary from the merely inquisitive to the positively ghoulish, history being littered with such instances. When in 1910 the two Scotland Yard officers who had arrested Dr Crippen and his mistress Ethel le Neve in Nova Scotia, docked at Liverpool, they were astonished to see over 4,000 people crowding the quay. Similarly in the 1920s and 30s, the great murder trials drew hundreds to the law courts, especially if advocates such as Marshall Hall, Henry Curtis Bennett, Norman Birkett or Patrick Hastings were involved in a case. In more recent times, crowds have flocked to the village of Lockerbie in the wake of the terrible plane disaster, and even to Soham after the dreadful murder of two little girls.

So it was with the Watkins case all those years ago. By the Sunday it was reported that huge numbers of people were arriving in order to view the 'murder house'. The inhabitants of Llangibby had never witnessed such scenes, for both The White Hart and The Fox and Hounds were having problems coping with the demand for ale. Some enterprising person had in fact set up two stalls and was selling buns, cakes, bananas, apples, pears, ginger beer and an assortment of sweets! The hot weather coupled with the over imbibing of the local beer and cider is a dangerous mix, and soon fights began to develop which rapidly deteriorated into mass brawls. The local police had to be called in to quell the commotion.

Police guarding the Watkins' cottage.

Away from Llangibby, where the Watkins cottage stood, even more disturbing acts were being committed. Obsessed souvenir hunters were grabbing whatever they could prise loose and remove from the area. They took stones from the garden path hopefully with traces of blood, tore pieces off the wicker gate, and even attempted to gain entry to the house. Their zealousness was partially repelled by a policeman being stationed outside of the front door, however when he left in the evening they ransacked the place. Eventually George Whitlock Nicholl, the owner had the entire place razed to the ground in the interests of safety. The site has since been ploughed over many times, but a careful inspection of the area still reveals the remains of small stone steps.

On Monday 22nd July, the petty sessions reconvened to hear more detailed accounts regarding the prisoner and the murders. This time even greater numbers of people gathered outside of the police station and the courthouse. The police had taken the sensible precaution of erecting barricades, but they were still uneasy. When the Chairman, Mr James arrived they were still battling to keep everyone at bay, and were indeed having great trouble in closing the courthouse doors. This proved too much for Mr James who addressing the overflow threatened to cancel the entire hearing unless order was restored. This had a salutary effect and they retreated from the room allowing the sessions hearing to begin.

It lasted almost three hours and consisted of the police being able to offer more definitive evidence about Garcia and his actions since leaving prison. Towards the end of these deliberations, the prisoner's solicitor Thomas Ensor rose to address the bench. Besides being a prominent solicitor, Ensor was also a Conservative Councillor in Cardiff, and when he died in 1895 his obituary stated that he was the first to have built a villa residence at Llanishen. In a speech of great eloquence he now expounded his belief in the importance of Garcia receiving a fair trial. Such was the effect of this address at the hearing that I have given it verbatum:

'I have appeared before you to watch the case on behalf of the prisoner by the instruction of the Spanish Consul for the Principality and Monmouthshire and I need hardly say a more painful duty has never devolved upon me. The prisoner has already been committed by warrant of the coroner to take his trial for the heinous offences which are laid to his charge and it is therefore comparatively indifferent to him what view the present tribunal may take of his case, for nothing probably will prevent a full and complete investigation of the matter before a jury at the Assizes.

I do not therefore propose to say one word on the subject of the prisoner's guilt or of the several witnesses who have disposed before you - I desire, on behalf of the gentleman who, at the instance of his Government, has requested me to watch the proceedings in the interest of the accused to express his unqualified abhorrence of the atrocious crime by whosoever committed, which has resulted in the cold blooded murder of no less than five individuals, without regard to age, sex or helplessness.

It is my hope and desire as it must be that of every well regulated mind, that the clear light of heaven may reveal the guilty perpetrator of these cruel and unprovoked atrocities, and that the sword of justice may smite with unerring aim. I have not a word of complaint to make against the loud, importunate and passionate cry for vengeance, which has pervaded the public mind on this unhappy occasion. Less was not to be expected. But, just the proportion as this appalling catastrophe and transcedent horrors, just in proportion as is the universal cry of 'blood for blood', so ought every effort to be made to clear up that which is mysterious and to withhold any judgement hostile to the accused, save on clear and irresistible evidence. It will, therefore, I think, be a matter of satisfaction to you and the public that this man will not be condemned unheard, and that, though an alien of blood and language, he will have provided for him, through the considerate liberality of his own Government, as full and ample means of making an answer to the charge preferred against him as if he had been an English subject. The excitement caused by this terrible tragedy, will I trust, speedily subside and when this awful and stupendous charge comes to be investigated by the tribunal to whose arbitratment it must be submitted finally, and in the last resort, I venture to predict that every antipathy and even the desire for vengeance itself will give way before that holier desire for the impartial administration of pure and simple justice which characterises English jurors even in the smallest concerns, and which attaches with ten fold weight when the issues are those of life and death. I trust that the 'Stranger and Sojourner' as well as the nationality to which they belong will never have cause to question the fairness and impartiality of English law and that, as in times past, so in these times present, and in times to come, this land may be regarded as none other than a sacred temple for the perpetual residence of an inviolable justice.'

The Chairman thanked him for his words before asking Senor Uncilla of the Spanish Legation who was present, to relay briefly the essence of the proceedings to the accused. This done Garcia was taken back to his cell, and the session ended.

As Garcia was now to stand trial at the Monmouth Assizes, he would have to be detained in Usk prison until the appointed date of the hearing. This was potentially a dangerous situation, as the volatile crowd would obviously be waiting either on the Caerleon-Usk road or outside of the prison itself. The local police decided that the best solution was to transport him in a horse-drawn 'fly and pair' taking the back road via Bulmore, Kemys Inferior and Llanllowell. This they succeeded in safely carrying out, much to their own and no doubt to Garcia's relief.

It must have seemed strange to the young Spaniard that he was back inside the very same prison that only a few days before had witnessed his release. He could also have wistfully reflected that if he had taken that rail ticket from George Whiting on the Tuesday morning he could well have been homeward bound by now.

The Crown Court hearing opened on Tuesday 31st July 1878 before Baron Pollock and the Grand Jury, whose foreman was Granville Somerset QC. The judge entered at 10.30 and for a few moments slowly surveyed all present, then in a quiet dignified voice he addressed the jury with the following remarks:

THE FEARFUL TRAGEDY AT LLANGIBBY.

MONMOUTHSHIRE ASSIZES.

CROWN COURT.—TUESDAY, JULY 30TH, 1878

Before BARON POLLOCK.

His Lordship took his seat at half-past ten o'clock, and the following gentlemen were empanelled as the

GRAND JURY:

Mr. Granville Somerset, Q.C., foreman; and Messrs. S. R. Bosanquet, H. C. Byrde, J. M. Bannerman, Richard Eastham, Thos. Falconer, Thos. Gratrex, G. R. Greenhow-Relph, George Griffin-Griffin, Jas. Graham, J. M. Herbert, J. Arthur Herbert, R. W. Hamilton, F. J. Hall, F. J. T. Amiel, John James, John D. James, H. M. Kennard, Edward Lister, George Lawrence, F. J. Mitchell, Francis M'Donnell, Richard Henry Oakley, and William Partridge.

'The number of prisoners in your calendar is not large, and with one terrible exception, you will have no difficulty in dealing with. There is one case, however, to which I have to call your attention, which, although not one of difficulty, so far as the facts are concerned, is certainly one which in its barbarity and in its cruelty is happily not only exceptional but, I think, it is one such as I myself have never before met with during the time I have had to administer the criminal law in this country.'

The judge then recounted the evidence of Miss Ann James who had twice passed the house on the evening the murders took place. He continued by outlining the release of Garcia from prison on that same day, of the prisoner's various movements afterwards, the eye witnesses, and his ultimate arrest the following night outside Newport railway station. Baron Pollock ended his address to the Grand Jury with these words:

'Gentlemen, this is a case, as I said before, so singular in its character, that I could not pass over details without mentioning them to you. As far as any difficulty you can have in dealing with this case, there really is none, because I am quite certain and have no doubt, whatever may be the result of the case, it will be your duty to find a true bill against this man for the offence with which he is charged.'

The Grand Jury then retired and on returning to the court passed a document to the Clerk of Arraigns. The latter announced, 'Gentlemen of the jury, you find a true bill against Joseph Garcia for murder.' The foreman bowed in agreement.

A silence descended on the court as Garcia was brought up from the cells and placed in the dock. His personal appearance had undergone a dramatic change during his time of confinement since the arrest. Gone was the natural olive complexion of the Spanish race, being replaced by a more leaden, bluish tint. There was a pinched look about his face the overall effect perhaps heightened by the vivid blue blouse that he wore. His demeanour had also noticeably altered, whereas at the sessions hearings he had been unaffected by the proceedings, now his face muscles twitched with a corresponding trembling around the mouth. His eyes darted to and fro as if he was unsure as to where or whom to focus upon. He appeared restless, and was extremely uneasy and anxious.

However his appearance in court was to be fairly brief as it was only then realised that Senor Uncilla, who was to act as interpreter, had not yet arrived. The judge decided to adjourn for lunch, so the prisoner was once more led away. Later, on reconvening with Uncilla present, Garcia was again placed in the dock. The Clerk of Arraigns asked the interpreter to put the question, 'Guilty or Not Guilty' to the prisoner. Garcia replied, in Spanish, 'Not Guilty'.

Mr S R Bosanquet QC with Mr A T Lawrence appeared for the Crown, whilst Mr Maddy, instructed by T H Ensor appeared for the defence. Mr Maddy was immediately on his feet to request that the trial be put back to the winter assizes in October at Gloucester. He stated that this was based on an affidavit prepared for him by Thomas Ensor, which offered three reasons for the postponement. The first was that the defence team had only received the depositions on the previous Thursday, and therefore had had little time to prepare their case for the prisoner. Again, as Garcia was Spanish and spoke little English, progress was obviously much slower when speaking to him through an interpreter, as it was imperative that he fully understood the seriousness of the charges against him.

Maddy emphasised that as the crime had naturally aroused such strong feelings in the county, it would be difficult to find an unbiased jury locally, whereas Gloucester would present no problems in that direction. Thus natural justice would not be interfered with in any way. The defence counsel added that when the prisoner was being brought into the present building, he was subjected to hissing and coarse invectives from those waiting outside. After Maddy had resumed his seat, Major Herbert was called who presented a letter he regarded as pertinent to the trial. This was handed to the judge and contained the statement that the prisoner was not the murderer, as the person who actually committed the crime had already left for Spain by ship from Newport Docks. The letter, which was addressed to the Newport borough police, was couched in the most abusive language, but was regarded by them as a simple red herring to add confusion to the case. It was signed with the name, 'Jimmy'.

The transfer of the trial of Garcia to Gloucester Winter Assizes was opposed by Bosanquet on the grounds that it was delay for delay's sake. There was now a considerable pause as Baron Pollock considered the defence counsel's request. Eventually the judge informed the court that he would have to confer with his colleague, Mr Justice Manisty, as the affidavit threw up a number of problems. On returning the judge decided to agree to a postponement, not however because of local feeling but on the grounds that the defence should be given adequate time to plead their case.

There was an odd postscript to the proceedings by reason of the low fees offered to those who had so far been involved in the case. Dr Donald Boulton, the Usk medical officer who had carried out the autopsies on the five members of the murdered family, and in addition had examined Garcia, was offended by the meagre payment of £3.19.6d. The analytical chemist Mr J W Thomas who had been employed from Cardiff, was so upset that he actually refused to accept the fee of £1.1.0d for his services.

Chapter Nine
'Innocence finds not nearly as much protection as guilt...'

Garcia spent the next three months incarcerated within Usk prison, during which time the local police undertook extensive searches in order to find the knife used in the attacks. Whilst he was in custody the warders observed that he would often stop working and gaze in an abstracted manner for some minutes at the ground, then heave a deep sigh, and once more resume his task. The forensic laboratory at Cardiff was carrying out numerous tests on Garcia's clothing as well as the items he had within the bundle when arrested. The excitement caused by the killings was now

Baron Bramwell.

losing its ghoulish appeal, and sightseers to the Llangibby area were slowly tailing off. Local auctioneers Philpot and Wingfield had been instructed to sell off the remaining items from the Watkins household, as a means of providing the surviving members of the family with some financial assistance. The auctioneers in respect of the cruelty of situation agreed to waive their fees.

The trial took place on Wednesday 30th October 1878 at Gloucester assizes under Baron Bramwell, the charge being 'the felonious killing of five members of the Watkins family'. The Crown was again represented by S R Bosanquet QC and Mr Lawrence, whilst the defence brief was given to Mr Gough QC and Mr Maddy, with a Mr Marquess acting as Spanish translator. Firstly the full details of the Crown's case against Garcia were expertly delivered by Bosanquet. He studiously outlined the events leading up to the murders and the subsequent discovery of the bodies of William and Elizabeth by the young Frank James.

Witness now followed witness into the box; prison warder George Whiting, Ann James, Frank James and John Evans all repeated the evidence they had previously given at the sessions hearing in Caerleon. The next to be called was John Morgan the

Gloucester Assizes.

farmer from Llangibby, who was questioned by Mr Lawrence. He asked him to relate to the jury the events of the morning of 17th July. This was Morgan's statement:

'I went to the cottage and saw the bodies of Watkins and his wife. I opened the door and went into the cottage. I looked round the room, and then I went upstairs to find the children. The room was full of smoke. I tried to find the

children, but I was obliged to go down to get my breath. Then I went for some water, and threw it where I saw the fire was. Then a man named Day came, and he ran to the furthest room and opened the window. He also dashed a hole through the roof. We then found the children. Two were in bed, one with his face downward. The third child was partly under the bed. All the children were dead.

There was not much blood about the lower room. I noticed the bodies of Watkins and his wife. There was blood where he lay, and on the door and on the gate. I did not see marks of a struggle. I don't know if it is a custom in this part to cover the faces of dead people with flowers.'

Thomas Day, innkeeper of 'The Fox and Hounds' at Llangibby, confirmed Thomas Morgan's version of events and added the following:

'About 8am on 17th July I went to the deceased's cottage. I broke a hole in the roof and opened the window, and thereby let the smoke out. I saw the three children dead. The bed was on fire, which was smouldering. I removed the bodies to the floor. While I was there Sergeant Povall arrived.'

Povall, who was stationed at Caerleon, now stepped into the witness box to be examined by Mr Lawrence. He was a key witness being the first police officer to arrive at the scene of the crime, and his testimony based on his diligent note-taking would be paramount to the prosecution's case. He gave the following account to the court:

'I went to the cottage at 9.30am on 17th July. I found Mrs Watkins lying in the garden near the gate. A little further on the body of William Watkins. The flowers were not then on his face. They had been pulled out of the bed. There was a great deal of blood where Mrs Watkins lay, as well as on the gate, and on the door. I saw footprints on the road from the side opposite the cottage. In one print there was a trace of blood, as of the right foot. It was from Mrs Watkins' body towards the road.

On the ground floor of the cottage I saw a number of things strewn about. In the corner of the room there had been a fire, and I saw the remains of charred linen. On the left hand side of the upstairs room there was the remains of another fire. A bed had been burnt. The three children were all laid dead side by side. The fires up and downstairs were all separate. On the table downstairs I saw some food, three rashers, some cold potatoes, the remains of a cup of tea, a knife and fork, and an awl.

I noticed two drawers, which had been ransacked, but contained some case knives. I found a baking tin, which I produce. There is a dent on the side and bottom. There was a frying pan on the floor with one little bit of bacon and some fat, and a kettle and a teapot on the table. There was also some fresh cut bacon on the floor. I found a hedge stake, also the weights, chain and pendulum of a clock in the midst of fragments of paper and other things.

In reply to further cross-examination, the sergeant answered:

'The clothes on the deceased were saturated with blood and there was indications of a severe struggle at the gate. The road is frequented by

51

persons from Usk and is an agricultural neighbourhood. There are not many tramps in Monmouthshire.'

In reply to questions from Judge Bramwell, Povall stated:

'The road is frequented by persons from Usk. It is an agricultural neighbourhood. The fire was out when I got there. The bed was burnt except for a small part in the middle.'

Sergeant McGrath of Newport police, who arrested Garcia outside the railway station, now gave his account:

'I examined the prisoner a little after midnight of the 17th of July. The prisoner had on the boots produced, two pairs of trousers - tweed and serge, tweed waistcoat, jacket, and hard bowler hat. Also the shirt produced. He had two bundles containing wearing apparel, blacklead pencil, kid gloves, shirtfront, three silk neckties, blacklead brush, and a number of other articles, including the works of a clock. The wearing apparel included articles worn by a man and a woman. There was also a piece of calico. A blue slop, cap and trousers were wet. The outside pair of trousers the prisoner had on were dry. The shirt had several stains on it. Part of the shirt had been washed. A loaf of bread showed the marks which corresponded with the tin (the baking tin of Elizabeth Watkins). A pocket knife, purse containing several coins. I did not ascertain the value of the coins.'

This was very damaging for the defence, as they needed to explain how so many of the articles from the Watkins household came to be in the possession of their client. For the moment Gough remained silent as Dr Boulton the Usk surgeon took the stand to give evidence with regard to the post mortems he had carried out on the five bodies. As he recited the results of his examination, the normal quietness of the court deepened into total and shocked silence. No rustling of papers, no coughing or fidgeting, no doors being opened or closed, even the very air of the room seemed to hang redolent upon his words. His dispassionate account only served to emphasise the full horror of the killings:

'I went to the cottage at 9.45am on the 17th. William Watkins's body was lying in the garden, dead. He was dressed except for his boots. Haemorrhage was the cause of death. There was a wound in his neck 5 inches deep. I saw Mrs Watkins's body. Her death was caused by a wound in the neck. There was also a second wound on the shoulder. A finger was out. I also saw the three children upstairs. The eldest, a girl aged 10, was wounded in the back of the neck. She died from haemorrhage. The boy died from wounds caused by stabs. The youngest was a girl, and she also had been stabbed. I made a post mortem examination of William Watkins's body. The stomach contained undigested food - bacon, beans, etc. He had evidently had a meal just before his death. The feet of two of the children were dislocated by the action of the fire.

I examined the prisoner on the 18th. I found several scratches across his face, as from thorns by going through a fence. Also marks on his left hand, about one inch in length. They were not cuts through the skin. In the cottage I noticed a child's dress with stains of blood upon it, as though a person had wiped his hands. I saw the prisoner's shirt and calico produced; they had bloodstains on them. Part of the shirt had the appearance of being wetted. The wounds could not have been self-inflicted.'

The visible effect of Dr Boulton's statement on the members of the jury is not of course difficult to imagine. Standing opposite to them was the prisoner Garcia, a stranger in their land, an alien, against which was aligned the most compelling of circumstantial evidence. This was perhaps the pivotal moment in the entire trial.

Cross-examined, Dr Boulton added the following:

'I should say that the scratches (on Garcia's face), had not bled. I believe that the wounds to the victims had been made with a sharper instrument than the knife found on the prisoner. It is not long enough to have produced a wound five inches deep. There was a wound on Watkins's forehead which might have produced insensibility.'

George Whiting, the Usk warder, was recalled to attest that there were no marks on Garcia's face or hands when he left prison, also stating that he had had no knife on him. Catherine Watkins, one of the surviving daughters of the deceased who was living at Glanusk at the time of the murders now identified a number of articles that had been in Garcia's possession at the time of his arrest, as belonging to her late father and mother. She also recognised a pair of stockings as her own, which she had left at her parent's house.

Mary Ann Watkins was questioned by Mr Lawrence; she answered as follows:

'I am the daughter of William Watkins. On the 15th July I left home to return to services. I left my father, mother, and two sisters and a brother at home well. I know the bag produced; it is marked 'S. Leigh'. It came from where I last lived. Mrs Leigh's. I know that the cloth jacket was my mother's. The coat was my father's; it was given him by the Rev. Mr Salisbury. The stockings produced belonged to a man for whom my mother washed. My father had a pair of black kid gloves. There was a clock in the house when I left on the 15th and also a bread tin.'

At the adjournment for lunch the prosecution announced that its case was now closed. On reassembling Mr Gough, no doubt to the bemusement of the Crown barristers, stated that there would be no evidence offered for the defence. It was a quite lamentable performance as little attempt had been made either to question or discredit the evidence given by the various witnesses. Bosanquet arose and ably and succinctly summed up for the prosecution.

Chapter Ten
'For whom the bell tolls,
It tolls for thee...'

Gough then offered his final plea on behalf of the prisoner. However his attitude and phrasing of delivery to the jury bordered on the uncertainty of the defeatist. In fact he began with the words, *'Gentlemen, I have a very difficult brief, a very difficult brief indeed'*, which was tantamount to resigning to the inevitable. He continued in the same vein:

> *'I am sure that you will agree with me that when we receive, through the public press, information of a frightful offence committed, such as that which forms the subject matter for inquiry today, there is not a human being who did not wish for full vengeance of guilt upon the person who committed that offence ... I appear on behalf of the prisoner today, not for one moment to extenuate or offer an excuse for the most diabolic offence ...'*

As a man's life was at stake, this is not the way to start if you wish to convince any jury that your client is not responsible for the indicted crime. He then offered the following for further digestion by the jury:

> *'There are a number of circumstances which tell most heavily against the unfortunate prisoner at the bar.'*

At this stage, Gough managed to offer some kind of defence for Garcia, but I suspect that the damage had already been done. After all, the court had listened to a veritable litany of descriptions of the most horrific nature, which would undoubtedly have brought revulsion to everyone present that day. The time for intensifying the atmosphere should certainly not be in the defence counsel's final address. Gough firstly offered the argument that in cases of suspicious circumstances, prejudice was a strong factor. He felt however that every accused person has his rights; warming to his subject he continued:

> *'You will feel it to be his right that if guilt should not be brought home conclusively to him, it is for you to say that the prosecution have failed in their endeavour. When crimes are committed you look for one thing, that is motive. If a man murders another, why does he do so? ... either from passion or anger, or for the sake of gain.*
>
> *Had he any reason for murdering Watkins? Would he have the heat or anger which would have led him to kill Watkins and then his wife? There is not the slightest proof that he had any spite against them, or the three poor children.*
>
> *Was he in want? He does not appear to have been in want. At the time of his arrest certain coins, both English and Spanish were found upon him. I would ask you to look at these coins, and you will see that they place him in a position above want.'*

Gough then proceeded to explain that Garcia possessed three pieces of gold which were at the time of his release from his nine month sentence, not appreciated by the Usk prison staff. He also emphasised that it was quite natural that the prisoner should have passed the day of his release idling away the hours asleep or dozing in the fields around Llangibby.

'There was no concealment by him. Do you think that a man committing a murder would be seen there, close by the place? Don't you think the intended murderer would hide and do everything to keep away from observation?'

He then reminded the jury that his client actually went to Mrs Gwatkin's to ask for a drink of water. At no time did he threaten her, attempt to rob her, but instead acted civilly with no sign of violent behaviour. Gough now turned to the damning evidence of the articles from the Watkins household and how they came to be in Garcia's possession. This was intended to be the focal point of the defence, and the barrister unfortunately showed that he was not really up to the task in hand.

'... the prisoner was close to the spot, that he went to the gate, and there saw these murdered people. The murderer heard steps approaching, and put down the articles which he had got ready for the purpose of removing, when the prisoner madly, foolishly, and greedily seized them. It may be that ... he thereby got some stains of blood on his clothes ... and tried to remove the stains.'

It sounded hollow to the listening court, and indeed was hollow. Not only that, it wasn't the brief that Thomas Ensor, Garcia's solicitor had given the barrister. The prisoner's story of how he acquired the stolen goods was totally different, although again it doesn't mean that the jury would have believed it. Yet it is obligatory that a barrister states his client's version of events, and not to concoct an alternative scenario. Gough now continued his defence speech:

'Do you believe that if he had committed the murder, and stolen these things he would for one instant have walked along to the railway station at Newport, that he might be found red-handed with these things in his possession? Do you think that he put on the clothes of the murdered man and walked along the road close to the house? Do you think it reasonable or likely that he would do anything of the kind?'

Gough's argument was to say the least rather tenuous. He was asking the jury to believe that Garcia would happily steal and wear the clothes of the William Watkins providing he had been murdered by someone else, but couldn't possibly do so if he himself had committed the crime. This is bordering on the preposterous. After questionning the illogicality of stealing parts of a clock, Gough emphasised that the prisoner was small in stature compared to Watkins so was unlikely to have overwhelmed him in a scuffle. He also brought to the jury's notice the lack of a weapon, and ultimately the lack of motive. Coming to the end of his address, he finished with:

'Supposing my theory be correct, here is a man to whom suspicion attaches because he is a discharged prisoner, carrying effects, and wearing the clothes of a murdered man, but there is an entire absence of motive. You have him in possession of money, coming straight to the police, and almost courting observation. And you are asked to say upon mere suspicion - strong I admit it to be - that he is guilty of the offence with which he is charged. What did he commit this offence for? Nothing is shown in his possession with which he could have committed this offence. Prejudice is strong, feeling is strong. Still there are some facts that speak most strongly. Have you any reasonable doubt? He is entitled to the benefit of that doubt. It is for you to say he is not guilty however strong the suspicion.'

With that Gough left the case in the hands of the jury. It was now time for Judge Bramwell to sum up the evidence of the case, and to direct the jury on points of law. He firstly advised them on one obvious point, that given the facts of the case there was no doubt that murder had been committed. Further, that it was for the prosecution to make out the guilt of the prisoner in the dock.

He explained that although the evidence was almost entirely circumstantial, that type of evidence could be so strong as to render a person as guilty as if you were actually witnessing the deed. Bramwell then added the following damning words:

> *'There is no doubt that the murderer was the thief. It is a rule of good sense, and one upon which juries always act, that when you find a man in possession of stolen property shortly after the theft has been committed, he is looked upon as the thief ... it is certain that the prisoner was in possession of stolen property.'*

Later on in his address he stated the following:

> *'Was the man murdered? If so was he not murdered by the prisoner? Is the prisoner not a thief? Has he got possession of the property, and not given an explanation of the way in which he came in possession of them? There is another thing. Blood is found upon his shirt partly washed off. There was none there when he left gaol. How did that get there?'*

Judge Bramwell appears to be quite dogmatic and unfortunately incorrect on certain points in his speech. Of course a doubt does exist as to whether the murderer was also the thief. It could of course be as Bramwell stated, but there certainly exists a doubt. Again he is incorrect when he says that Garcia hasn't given an explanation of how he came to have the stolen items. Gough's version, although differing from his client's, is still a matter of trial record which the judge seems to have forgotten. The most glaring error in his statement revolves around the bloodstained shirt. The Cardiff analyst gave evidence to the effect that the stain was not of recent origin. The judge eventually ended his address to the jury with the following words:

> *'You are the judges of the facts in this case. Did this man murder William Watkins? If you are satisfied, although no one saw him do it, you ought, you must pronounce it. That which goes against him is this. The cottage was robbed, and the stolen property found upon the prisoner, and he can give no account of it. If you are satisfied that the thief and the murderer are the same person, then you must say he is guilty. This is a matter of very great importance to society at large.'*

After a judicial summing up of that nature, it is not surprising, even though a man's life was at stake, that the all male jury never left their box, but merely conferred between themselves. After two or three minutes discussion, the foreman arose to announce that they had reached a verdict. To a hushed court he was asked by the clerk to state their decision, to which he replied that they found the prisoner guilty of murder. Although this was immediately conveyed to Garcia via an interpreter, he remained unmoved and still appeared to show little interest in the proceedings. The 'black cap' was now placed upon Judge Bramwell's head, and he intoned the fatal words that would consign the prisoner to the gallows. However, whether deliberately or by error, he omitted to say the final words, *'May God have mercy on your soul.'*

The date of execution was fixed for Monday 18th November, and Garcia was then taken below before being transferred back to Usk gaol, and the condemned cell. Initially a degree of numbness or disbelief at the verdict no doubt exists, but as the days pass this would gradually give way to fear and even terror, as the prospect of the hanging draws ever nearer. Interestingly, Albert Pierrepoint, the most famous executioner of the twentieth century, remarked in his autobiography, that it was unusual for a prisoner to baulk or struggle at the sight of the scaffold and the noose. Although he only met the condemned person minutes before the hanging, he alluded to their often astonishing composure in the face of impending doom.

Guilty verdict on Garcia.

Joseph Garcia was now a very different man to the one released on that bright morning in mid-July. Broken in spirit, pinched in features, with a visible weight loss, he remained for the most part lost in his thoughts. Unable to converse with the two ever-present warders, his silence must have been equally irksome to them. Naturally the days that follow between the sentence of the court and the actual moment of execution are the most arduous for the prisoner, and perhaps to those wishing revenge on such a person a deserving part of their punishment.

It was at this stage however that a series of extraordinary events occurred, which to an extent offers a clue to the debates that continue to this day with regard to Garcia's guilt. Although the circumstantial evidence was of course overwhelming, and the jury had little hesitation in coming to their verdict, Thomas Ensor, the prisoner's solicitor was extremely upset by what he considered to have been a quite incompetent performance by the defence counsel Gough. In his eyes it amounted to a gross dereliction of duty.

It was Ensor's opinion that Gough made only feeble and ineffectual attempts to expound his client's version of events, and by changing that version was an abject admission of defeat. Ensor now conveyed his serious misgivings to Senor Uncilla of the Spanish Legation, which resulted in a joint letter of appeal to the Home Department, the latter being the Victorian equivalent of today's Home Office. They requested a review of the entire case, and of the trial proceedings at Gloucester. This met with no success, in fact the Home Department deigned not to reply!

However events now took a dramatic twist in the form of the Crown Prosecutor, S R Bosanquet. He himself was profoundly disturbed at the trial proceedings, and this led him to the extraordinary decision to visit Usk gaol and through an interpreter converse with Garcia. The result of these discussions only served to increase his disquiet, the eventual outcome being that Bosanquet decided to write himself to the Home Department relating his own unease at the outcome of the trial. This action by a barrister who has already gained the verdict must be unique in the annals of legal proceedings. It forced the hand of the Home Department, but unlike present day procedures, where the Home

Secretary with his advisers investigate, in those days it was simply a matter of writing to the judge in charge of the trial, in this case Baron Bramwell, and enquire as to his opinion. Bramwell replied that he had no doubt that the decision of the jury was sound. This effectively sealed Garcia's fate.

The condemned cell in which Garcia spent his final days is still in use to this day, being number one cell on the first floor. When I was recently invited to visit Usk prison I found that it now has two bunk beds, a screened off toilet, a desk and chair, and high up on the wall opposite the cell door a barred window, the latter comprised of small individual panes of thick glass.

As the autumnal days inexorably gave way to the twilight of winter, so Garcia's constitution likewise deteriorated. With a poor appetite, and surviving only on beef tea and bread, he visibly lost weight, becoming almost unrecognisable to the man who had strolled through Usk on that bright July morning when first released from confinement. Yet he still did not appear capable of understanding the awful position he was in, and simply did not believe that he was going to be executed. During the last two weeks of his life he received numerous visits from Senor Uncilla and the Roman Catholic priest, Father Echavarria.

At early evening on Friday 15th November a small neatly attired man carrying a large suitcase stepped off the last train to arrive that day at Usk station. He made his way unobserved through the town until he was quietly let in at the prison gates. His name was William Marwood, and he was the Newgate executioner. On Saturday 16th November Garcia was visited by the High Sheriff of Monmouth, John C Hanbury of Pontypool, together with the Under Sheriff Edmund B Edwards, Senor Uncilla and his assistant Senor de Angullo of Newport. They stayed with him for nearly half an hour, hoping that having a large number of people in his cell would induce the prisoner to confess his guilt, but to no avail. He simply denied any involvement whatsoever.

On the Sunday, the day before the appointed date of execution Uncilla again visited Usk gaol in the company of his assistant de Angullo. Perhaps for the first time Garcia now showed that he understood his predicament, as he broke down in tears and threw his arms around the Consul's neck. He passionately insisted on his innocence, repeating over and over again that he hadn't done it. As the distraught Consul eventually left, Fr. Echavarria arrived to offer comfort to the prisoner. The priest in a moment of compassion got on his knees and kissed the feet of Garcia, imploring him to confess his guilt in the sight of God. The prisoner raised the priest to his feet and firmly responded, 'No, I am innocent.' Weeping bitterly he cried out, 'They are going to kill me for what I have not done. Oh! My mother and sister!'

The Reverend Father then administered the Last Sacraments of the Church, and after offering spiritual advice, Garcia was asked to make his confession. He did so, but not to the murders of the Watkins family. The Reverend Father later was to say that Garcia's greatest wish was to see his mother, and the thoughts of never again having the opportunity of seeing her face caused him intense grief. One of his last requests was that his parents should be written to and to tell them, 'that I die innocent.'

Joseph Garcia spent his last night on earth in the company of two warders, Henry Coward and Joseph Olroyd. The events of that night have been the subject of much discussion, including an internal prison inquiry. This arose through the Western Mail printing a rather fanciful account of how these two warders had threatened and conjoled Garcia into admitting that he had carried out the murders. The article also related that Coward and Olroyd had woken up the prisoner on the hour throughout the night to inform him as to how long he had to live! The truth seemed to have been that Garcia himself had requested that they should rouse him every so often and tell him the time.

Whatever the degree of visciousness of the crime committed, the hour of retribution, that is the actual execution, exerts enormous stress on all the participants, except perhaps the hangman himself. At 5am on the morning of Monday 18th November 1878, a special Mass was said at Usk Catholic Church, led by the local priest Fr. Croft, and attended by Fr. Echavarria. At its completion the two priests slowly, and no doubt with considerable apprehension, made their way to the prison.

As early as seven o'clock a crowd was already beginning to form outside of the gaol, with many trying to gain a view of the scaffold by occupying high vantage points. I suppose little changes in the way of human nature, as this uncomfortably repeats the scenes earlier described by Dickens and Thackeray. Even in the twentieth century, there was always a large number of people standing outside of the prisons on the morning of executions.

Inside Usk gaol, the appointed officials had by now gathered, with Marwood making last minute adjustments to the hang rope, and of course testing the efficiency of the trap door mechanism. The six reporters allowed into the prison, were now ushered into a small room where they had their names entered in the gatekeeper's visitors book. They were then taken to view the already dug grave that awaited the condemned prisoner's body. It was sited in the exercise ring at the south-east side of the gaol, which meant that the other prisoners would pass over it during their exercise periods. The grave was roughly ten feet deep, but as this was below water level, it already held nearly twelve inches of water. This would be removed before burial. Next Marwood conducted them to the scaffold which was made of deal and painted black. In fact the scaffold and gibbet wasn't the property of Usk prison, but was stored at Reading gaol, from where it was transported and reassembled at each place of execution. He explained to them the sequence of the hanging, where he would use a length of rope of eleven feet, which would give an eight feet drop.

At precisely twenty minutes to eight a lone church bell began to toll the funeral knell over the silent town. This monstrous sound, which added solemnity to the scene, suddenly ceased a quarter of an hour later. It is this single ringing that gives rise to the phrase, *for whom the bell tolls*. The large crowd outside of the gaol likewise fell silent, waiting, waiting. At five minutes to eight a small group of officials including the two priests made their way to the pinioning room, to which Garcia had already been taken. Marwood entered and at his first sighting of his executioner Garcia almost collapsed. As his arms were strapped to his side, Garcia whispered to Fr. Echavarria, 'I go now?' The priest replied quietly, 'No, no. Courage; you shall know the moment.'

After a short pause, he was taken to the door that led to the scaffold. Leading the way was the deputy-governor, C W Usherwood with Marwood, then Garcia, whose feeble and tottering figure was supported by warders Whiting and Powell. Next came Fr. Croft reading the funeral service, and by his side Fr. Echavarria holding aloft a crucifix. The under-sheriff Major Herbert, Drs J Boulton and D Boulton; the chaplain to the prison Rev. J Cadwallader and six warders brought up the rear. All took up positions around the scaffold.

Garcia who had taken on a sickening appearance, was dressed in a blue guernsey, a pair of policeman's trousers and boots, with a grey flannel shirt underneath the guernsey. Supported by the two warders, his eyes firmly closed, he was placed on the stage of the scaffold. Fr. Echavarria stepped forward and held his crucifix to

Garcia's lips and kissed it twice. The condemned man looked skywards and uttered the words, 'Jesu, Jose, Maria.' Marwood quickly placed the noose around his neck, tightened, and pulled a white hood over the head. The suspense had almost reached breaking point as the executioner pulled the scaffold bolt to release the trap door mechanism, sending Joseph Garcia plunging down into the pit, and his soul into eternity.

PORTRAIT of GARCIA THE LLANGIBBY MURDERER.

The execution party was stricken into horrific silence as the body of the young Spaniard convulsed on the rope for over two minutes, until it finally became still. The white-faced officials filed away leaving only Marwood who remained for a while gazing at the inert body. In keeping with tradition a black flag was immediately hoisted above the prison entrance. It contained a single word in large white letters, 'Justice'. At the sight of this, the considerable crowd waiting outside went into a frenzy of jubilation, with wild cheering and clapping. Within the prison Dr Boulton, after the mandatory hour, entered the pit and after examining the body, pronounced Garcia dead. He then carried out an autopsy before the body was buried within the grounds.

Marwood on leaving the gaol at around 1pm, received a tumultuous reception from a highly excited crowd. They eagerly pressed forward, each wanting to shake his hand or clap him on the back, for a job well done. The scene took on the atmosphere of a village carnival, as he was bodily escorted firstly to the Crown Inn where toasts were offered to his good health, and then on to The Three Salmons hotel. Eventually he managed to reach the railway station, and as the train pulled away was given three rousing cheers from the crowded platform.

The Pontypool Free Press commented in undisguised disgust:

> *'We feel it would be wrong to omit mention of other scenes, in connection with this execution, which are almost more dreadful than the awful scene itself; and we believe all right-minded people will agree with us in thinking that they are, in some measure, a sort of disgrace to the county. We mean the ovations accorded Marwood, the excecutioner at Usk and Pontypool Road, at which places crowds of people vied with each other in drinking with him, shaking him by the hand, and congratulating him upon his work that day.'*

Chapter Eleven
'I say I am a man, but who is this that hides inside of me...'

So the story has come full circle, from the moment that a young Spanish sailor arrived unknown in a foreign land to the day he met his early death on a scaffold in Usk. The Watkins family had been decimated, a father mother and three young children slaughtered in a night of brutal and sickening violence. Yet the tiny seed of doubt that was partially created by the actions of Ensor and Bosanquet has persisted down the years. Its light has burned steadily, never brightly, but enough to give pause to those who have taken an interest in the case.

Although, as is frequently the case, there was obviously no direct witness to the murders, the degree of circumstantial evidence was extremely strong and convincing. Yet Judge Bramwell's comment that such evidence is almost the equivalent of being there, is not strictly true. This was tragically demonstrated some seventeen years later in the astonishing case of Adolf Beck.

This gentleman was walking down Victoria Street in London on 16th December 1895, when he was accosted by a Madame Meissonier, who accused him of defrauding her of a considerable amount of money. A nearby policeman was called, and he escorted both of them to the nearest station, where after hearing the lady's complaint, they promptly arrested Beck. Within a short space of time several other women came forward to attest that this was the very man who had also duped money out of them. In the face of such irrefutable evidence, given by respectable women, Beck was later found guilty and jailed for seven years.

After serving his sentence, he was astonishingly charged again for committing the same offence, and once more found guilty. The judge however deferred sentencing, and during that time a John Smith, alias William Wyatt, was caught carrying out similar crimes. It was then that one of the senior police officers noticed the extraordinary likeness between Smith and Beck, and realised the terrible mistake that had occurred. Poor Adolf Beck was immediately released with a full pardon, but it had broken his spirit and he died only a few years later.

Thus it can be seen that evidence that comes under the heading of circumstantial, should also involve circumspection. In the case of Joseph Garcia, a number of questions arise, some answerable, others forever lost in the mists of time. In an attempt therefore to try to clarify the crime and the moments leading up to the killings, I have tried to reconstruct them, in one the case Garcia being guilty, and in the other innocent.

1. *Garcia: Guilty As Charged*
It is well documented that he spent the Tuesday, the day of his release from prison, idling or sleeping in fields adjacent to the Usk - Llangibby - Caerleon road. As evening approached the sightings cease, yet with the coming darkness he is still wandering the surrounding countryside. It must be remembered that he had spent the last nine months sleeping in a prison cell, a roof over his head, whereas now he is in the open air. It must have been a strange experience for him to see the blackness of night approaching, with the curious and slightly unnerving sounds that accompany it. In those days there was no street lighting, so the night would eventually become absolute.

Perhaps this prompted him to try to find a place to stay, to seek shelter. In the gathering gloom he follows the road from Llangibby until he sees a tiny yellow light shining from a window in an isolated house by the wayside, the house belonging to the Watkins family. Garcia opens the gate and walks up to the door and knocks on it. William Watkins, tired from his day's labour, is roused from his supper, and on opening the door he finds himself confronted by the small, bedraggled figure of Joseph Garcia. He sees a foreigner, an olive skinned man of dirty appearance, who attempts in broken English and perhaps gesticulations to ask for food and a bed for the night.

Xenophobia was certainly rife in those far off days, as even people from different villages were sometimes treated with suspicion and prejudice. Perhaps Garcia was gruffly told to go away and to get off the property. William, who was a strong man by dint of his hard working life, might even have physically forced him towards the gate. Garcia was of Iberian blood, hot and easily aroused to rage, so when William turned to go back to his house, the Spaniard might have picked up a loose stave and in blind fury struck him down. This would offer an explanation for the wound found on Watkins' forehead during the post mortem of Dr Boulton.

The labourer falls full length on the path, semi-conscious, and his moans quickly brings out his wife Elizabeth to see what all the noise is about. Garcia likewise attacks her and she similarly is rendered insensible. He now enters the house, picks up a kitchen knife and returning to the path, viciously stabs to death the two prostrate victims. Proceeding to ransack the kitchen he might then have overheard the children upstairs, or alternatively perhaps he mounted the stairs to see if there was anything worth stealing, only to be suddenly confronted by them. To avoid being identified as the killer of their parents, he uses the knife to murder them as well. Before vanishing into the night carrying his booty, he attempts to set fire to the house in order to cover up his crimes and also stops to remove the shoes of William Watkins. Twenty four hours later he is arrested outside Newport railway station by Sergeant McGrath and PC Tooze.

This, I think you will agree, is a very plausible scenario, and one I surmise was approximate to that in the minds of the jury when they pronounced Garcia guilty. However there are still a number of interesting questions that arise from it. These questions do not in any way discredit this version of events, but I believe are still pertinent to establishing the truth.

1. *What was the point of Garcia setting fire to the house, when the bodies of the parents were lying outside on the garden path?*

2. *He was arrested after PC Tooze eventually recognised him from the description issued by Usk prison staff. As Garcia had received an exemplary report from warder George Whiting on completion of his sentence there, why was he singled out as a possible suspect when other prisoners were released at the same time?*

3. *It is conceivable that Garcia would, before making his escape, stop to remove William Watkins' boots, as this was an act of profit. Yet it does seem implausible that he would also take the time to pull Sweet William flowers from the garden and place them over the dead man's face.*

4. *In the 24 hours that elapsed before his arrest in Newport he was never once sighted, though he made little effort to leave the area. Surely the normal reaction of someone in that predicament is to get as far away as humanly possible, and in the shortest time?*

5. *Although there were spots of blood on Garcia's shirt, they were according to the Cardiff analyst, not of recent origin. Given that he*

killed two adults and three children by the most savage and bloody means, surely he would have been drenched in blood? Not just his shirt, but his trousers, under his finger nails, and even on the bundle he so rapidly assembled before departing the scene of crime. Yet the only mention of contamination is on the shirt, but only because it was damp, and therefore had been assumed to have been washed. Could you remove such gross stains by simply immersing it in a nearby brook?

6. *It is strange that he doesn't appear to have eaten anything for the best part of two days. Yet no doubt suffering from intense hunger pangs, he still had not touched the loaf of bread he stole from the Watkins cottage when arrested. Was this because he didn't know it was in the bundle?*

7. *Between the time he was first observed by PC Tooze to the second sighting outside Newport railway station, Garcia made no attempt to flee, or indeed to get rid of the incriminating bundle of items from the Watkins household.*

8. *The surviving members of the Watkins family readily identified the items that Garcia had with him as belonging to their family. As it had already been indicated by Dr Boulton that the knife found on Garcia was not the murder weapon, where did he find such an implement? The obvious answer is from the kitchen of the house, yet none of the family stated that a knife was missing.*

All of these of course are mere questions and not answers. Yet it demonstrates the incompetence of Gough that he failed to promote so few of them in his so called defence of his client. It is therefore understandable why Garcia's solicitor, Thomas Ensor should have been so appalled at the barrister's performance, and why he decided to try, although unsuccessfully, to lodge an appeal against the verdict.

2. Garcia as Innocent Victim
We now turn to the alternative scenario, for if Garcia was not responsible for these murders, then who was? If it is accepted that the three bastions that lead ultimately to murder are greed, lust or hatred, it is worthwhile attempting to see which of these fit into the Watkins case. It has already been remarked that the killings could not have occurred for the simple aim of robbery, as the rewards were so insignificant. This is a fallacy, as many people over the years have been killed for next to nothing.

If indeed hatred was the motive, who might be involved? As the police never extended their investigations beyond the search for Garcia, we have no information with regard to the household situation of the Watkins's. There may have been family problems, as indeed the majority of murders arise from domestic conflicts, although in this case there is no evidence to support such a claim. However it is worth mentioning here that a curious article appeared in The South Wales Argus of May 1994, when a William Watkins of Newport claimed to be the grandson of an illegitimate child born from an affair between Garcia and Mary Ann Watkins, the eldest daughter of the Watkins family! She was one of the fortunate members who was not present on the night of the murders. The writer claimed that Garcia had met and fallen in love with Mary Ann a year before he was imprisoned for burglary. The latter was a direct result of the need by Garcia to obtain money to support Mary Ann and the child.

He further claimed that on Garcia's release from prison some nine months later, he went to the home of William Watkins in the hope that he could be reconciled with Mary Ann. However her father rebuffed him and angrily attempted to throw the young Spaniard off his property. Garcia flew into a rage and proceeded to kill everyone there that night. It has to be admitted that this seems to be highly unlikely, as firstly Mary Ann would have been only fifteen, and during the trial period no mention was ever made of it, either by the young girl or by anyone else in the village.

The advent of tramps in the area was not unknown and often as night approached they would take refuge in each other's company. Could Garcia's story of how he came by the stolen goods be actually true? Did tramps break in, overpower the parents, and after having slain the children to prevent identification, panicked and fled the scene. In their haste did they simply throw away the bundle of looted items?

If this was the case, the question of where and when Garcia found the discarded bundle was never discussed, as his barrister insisted on stating that his client had actually disturbed the real murderer at the scene. As previously noted, Thomas Ensor has emphasised that this was not Garcia's own version of the events of that night. So if he had found them as indicated, then it was either on the roadside or possibly the far side of one of the hedges. It might also explain why he didn't know that it contained a loaf of bread.

Taking this a step further, if the Spaniard slept innocently in a field throughout the night, when exactly did he come upon the bundle? It is unlikely that he would have seen it during the hours of darkness, so it must have been sometime during the Wednesday. There are a great many fields and deep lanes in that part of Gwent, and with a correspondingly low level of population, it is hardly surprising that he went unnoticed for long periods of time.

We now come to perhaps the one incident which has cast the most doubt over Garcia's guilt; namely the actions of the Crown prosecutor S R Bosanquet. He was obviously deeply troubled over the entire affair, but what exactly was the basis of his concern. It could be argued that the fairness of the trial left something to be desired, as Garcia would obviously have had little understanding of much of the cross examinations, or indeed his own barrister's arguments. This would of course explain why he showed such little interest in the proceedings. Again the poor performance of Gough offered little in the way of an adequate defence.

Bosanquet would have observed all of this and perhaps his own personal high standard of conduct prompted him to visit Garcia in an attempt to gain the truth of the matter. However if he was only concerned with establishing to his own satisfaction the prisoner's guilt then I suspect that he would have let things be. The court proceedings might well be questionned, but at least the verdict was correct. Yet it was after his visit to Usk prison that the barrister wrote his letter of concern to the Home Department. Was he now genuinely alarmed or at the least troubled by the conviction of Garcia? Did his conversations with the prisoner, via an interpreter confirm his worst fears? We shall never know, but it certainly adds a new and mysterious element to the case.

Over 125 years have now passed since that fateful night in the summer of 1878, so it seems that little more will be gleaned about the crime. All the participants and even their immediate descendants are no longer with us, so we are left to the mercy of rumour and gossip. These have always tended to side with the controversial, with the possibility that established facts are somehow tarnished and some great wrong has occurred. Naturally this is always more exciting than the mere mundane but logical explanation. The events of that fateful date in 1878 are now themselves being slowly buried under the silt of time. The old folk of Llangibby have passed down their memories to their children, but with each successive generation the telling becomes more dilute, more distorted.

The evidence against the young Spaniard, although circumstantial, was obviously strong. In basic terms, he was seen in the vicinity of the Watkins cottage, he had articles and clothing from the cottage, and he was an ex-prisoner convicted of burglary, ergo he was the monster who committed those dreadful acts. Yet, and I pause, yet the possibility certainly exists that his version of events was true, and that he became unknowingly entrapped in a bizarre situation that would lead him inevitably to the gallows.

We shall never know the real truth that lies behind the killings, but one final question still stands to this day. When Marwood the executioner placed the noose around the neck of Joseph Garcia on that grey Monday morning, was he hanging an innocent man?

Addendum

There were four surviving members of the Watkins family, so what did the future hold for them? Mary Ann Watkins, who so bravely gave evidence at the trial, eventually married and moved to Vinegar Hill in Undy where she died many years later. William Jasper Watkins was living in the village of Magor at the time of the murders. He was to die there. Catherine Watkins, who was in service in London for many years, returned to Wales, living at Barry at the time of her death. Arthur Watkins moved to Pontypool to become an employee of the Hanbury Tenison family. He was initially a groom but advanced to the post of Coachman before, in 1922, the family transferred to Park Estate at Pontymoile. Arthur and his family went with them. His son was named Frederick, perhaps in memory of Arthur's young brother who died that night in the summer of 1878.

Arthur Watkins descendant of the Watkins family.

As to the family of Joseph Garcia, little is known about them. However a few years ago a visitor to Llangibby asked the local vicar if he might inspect the church records regarding the Watkins family. Astonishingly this person turned out to be a descendant of Garcia, and had travelled from Spain specifically to see where it had all happened. In fact he had already been to the prison at Usk and had been shown the condemned cell where his ancestor had spent his final days. He also wanted to see the place where Garcia had been buried. Unfortunately this was not possible for all the prisoners who had either been executed or died whilst serving their sentences, had been buried in a strip of land adjacent to the south wall of the prison. Today this area is occupied by a wide border filled with shrubs and flowers, with no indication where each individual was positioned.

Today the village of Llangibby, like Usk, has experienced a gradual increase in land development. Although a significant number of new houses have appeared, it maintains to a degree its geographical isolation, but modern transport has certainly had an impact. Local worshippers still attend the old church of St Cybi's, its ancient walls resisting the cold blasts of winter and the rains of summer. The surrounding cemetery, appropriately overgrown, holds the grave of the Watkins family, its stone monument now weather beaten and ingrained with lichen. A rhododendron shrub has grown alongside, its branches and leaves offering a cool canopy when the heat of July arrives each summer. A July that witnessed many years ago perhaps the saddest day of all as mourners laid to rest William, Elizabeth, Charlotte, Alice and Frederick Watkins. The inscription on the headstone can still be discerned, although Charlotte's age is given incorrectly:

In
Memory of
WILLIAM WATKINS Aged 39
His Wife ELIZABETH Aged 40
Greatly respected.
Who with their children
CHARLOTTE, ALICE and FREDERICK
Aged respectively 9, 5, and 4 years
Were cruelly murdered
July 16th 1878
'Not one of them is forgotten Amen'

And what of the house, the 'murder house' as the locals once called it? Nothing remains today. On a recent walk with David Husband who lives at Llangibby I was shown the place where he believes the house and garden once were. As you travel out of the village and breast the rise, the road curves slightly, and on the right you can see a field in the shape of a small hillock. It is thought that the house once stood at the base of this field, where there is an observable flattening of the ground. The road that existed in Victorian times and passed in front of the Watkins' cottage has changed, so it is not easy to be sure of the exact site. The old road was lower and has been radically built up to the level we see today.

On the opposite side, about six feet below the road is a wooden stile. The locals recall that it was on this very stile that a stranger sat on the morning of Tuesday 16th July 1878. A small band of young children approached from the direction of Newbridge-on-Usk but on seeing this person they retreated in some fear. Older children then accompanied them back, and the stranger, Joseph Garcia, allowed them to pass!

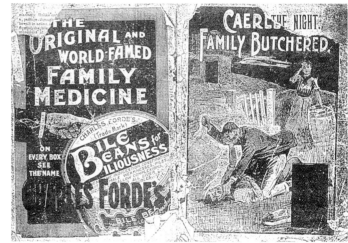

These days traffic between Usk and Caerleon passing through Llangibby accelerate up the incline out of the village with never a glance at the small field on their right. Most are oblivious of the tragedy that was played out so long ago. Perhaps it is as well.

Appendix 1

The following is a poem composed on 24th July 1878, by Julia M Highley of Cwmbran.

First Picture
A quaint old town, a peaceful-flowing river,
A grand old castle, ivy-clad and grey,
A gloomy gaol - and from its frowning portals
Steps a young stranger, whose lithe form and olive-tinted skin
Speak of a home in sunny lands afar,
An outcast he is in our land.

In vain he seeks a pitying eye:
All shun the felon wretch;
None offer him a cup of water in the Master's name,
He leaves the pretty town with frightful curses,
His heart full of a bitter deadly hate.
"Revenge!" he shrieks in fury, and his eyes
Gleam with a baleful light on all he meets,
Yet craftily he bides his time like an Indian Thug,
To fully glut the insatiate Fiend Revenge!
Great God! Is there no pity in his heart
That should haste to slay the innocent?
Are there no tender memories to bring a softened light to those wild eyes?
Is there no rush of blinding tears, like summer rain,
To cool the lava passions of his soul? …
Ah, could he but recall the vine-wreathed cot,
The sunny slopes where luscious muscatels,
In cluster rich display their dewy bloom,
That mountain path, how oft his childish steps
Have follow'd to the shrine his mother.
There, kneeling, she would pray with all,
A mother's love, heaven's blessing on her boy
O fatal gulf
That separated him from days of happy innocence!
O could he but have known, when first he sail'd away,
That he had look'd his last on that dear face,
Bath'd in a flood of tears, because her boy -
Her only one - resisted all her pleadings,
And would sail across the main:
He had look'd his last, for ever,
On the sunny land of Spain!

Second Picture
An English village at the close of day.
The setting sun bathes in its rosy light the happy cottages homes,
The windows and the gardens gay with summer flowers;
And children's merry voices, in their happy play,
Mingle with merry mowers' song among the new-mown
A little later, and their toil was o'er;
Each sought his home, and wives rejoiced
To hear a manly step paused tiredly at the door.
See, yonder is a humble whitewash'd cot -
The light within streams o'er the dusty road;
The savoury smell of humble cottage fare
And cheerful hum of voices are like drieriest mockery
To the foot-sore wand'rer who stands without;
And later still, the moon shines forth in undimm'd splendour:
Her tender light falls with a soften'd gleam
Upon the silent cot and distant village church,
Where the forefathers of the hamlet sleep -
And, creeping mid the shadows steathily,
A human monster flees away,
Drunk with a carnival of blood.

Third Picture

The dawn breaks softly, and the sun shines forth,
Revealing the dread secrets of the night
By gentle Luna hid.
The garden trim - so late the pride
Of these poor honest hearts now lying stark and cold,
Whose life blood mingling with the summer flowers
Mutely demands that vengeance should be taken
For this foul deed.
And in the humble home three helpless babes,
Wrapp'd in the happy sleep of childhood, wake
To hear the death-shriek of their parents rend
The calm still night.
O scene to make an angel weep;
Their little forms
Are hack'd and hew'd beneath the assassins stroke,
Till mercifully, death releases them,
And their martyr'd spirits - angel-attended
Enter the realms of never-ending bliss
To dwell for ever with our glorious King,
Who when on earth, in accents meek and mild,
Welcom'd as meet for heav'n a little child.

Appendix 2

DECLARATIONS OF THE SHERIFF
AND OTHERS.

---

31 Vict.   Cap. 24.

We the undersigned, hereby declare that

Judgement of Death was this day executed on

_____ in His Majesty's Prison of

_____ in our presence.

Dated this _____*day of* _____

_____Sheriff of _____

_____ Justice of the Peace

for _____

_____Governor of the said Prison

_____ Chaplain of the said Prison

Appendix 3

Autopsy Report by Dr James Boulton Given at Inquest

William Watkins: Aged 39.   *5" deep knife wound severed jugular and carotid artery - laying bare 2nd and 3rd vertebrae.*

Elizabeth Watkins: Aged 40.   *Similar throat and neck wounds.*

Charlotte Watkins: Aged 8.   *Scorched body, and knife wounds to neck.*

Alice Watkins: Aged 5.   *Unrecognisable due to massive burns to the face - right toes burned away.*

Frederick Watkins: Aged 4.   *Throat cut, left foot severely burned and ankle dislocated.*

Appendix 4

The following is the post mortem results carried out by Dr Boulton on the body of Joseph Garcia, one hour after the execution.

POST MORTEM EXAMINATION RESULTS

EXTERNAL EXAMINATION

Marks of violence, Identification etc.	Deep impression around neck of noose with suspension point about 1" in front of the angle of the left lower jaw. Vital changes locally and in the tissues beneath as a consequence of sudden constriction. No ecchymoses in the face - or, indeed elsewhere. No marks of restraint.
How long dead?	One hour.

INTERNAL EXAMINATION

Skull, brain, meninges.	Fracture discolation of the spine at C.2 with 2" gap and transverse separation of the spinal cord at the same level.
Mouth, Tongue & Oesaphagus	Fractures of both wings of the hyoid and the right wing of the thyroid cartilage. Larynx also fractured.
Liver and Gall Bladder	Terminal congestion only.
Kidney & Ureters	Slight terminal congestion only.

OTHER REMARKS Deceased was healthy subject at the time of death. Mark of suspension normally situated and injuries from judicial hanging - to the spinal column and cord - such as must have caused instant death.

CAUSES OF DEATH Injuries to the central nervous system consequent upon judicial hanging.

Appendix 5

INSTRUCTIONS TO BE OBSERVED IN BURYING THE BODIES OF EXECUTED PRISONERS

1. *All clothing with the exception of shirt or similar garment, will be removed from the body, which will be placed in a coffin made of 1/2" wood, deal or pine.*

2. *The sides and ends of the coffin will be well perforated with large holes.*

3. *Lime will not be used.*

4. *The original size of the plot of ground will be 9 ft. by 4 ft., and the Grave will be from 8 to 10 ft. in depth.*

5. *When the coffin has been covered with 1 foot of earth, charcoal to the depth of three inches will be thrown into the grave, which will then be filled in. The top coffin will be not less than 4 feet below the ground surface.*

6. *Arrangements will be made for the grave sites to be used in sequence.*

7. *A register of graves will be kept, containing the name of each convict buried, the date of burial, the site of the grave, and the position of the coffin in the grave.*

PART THREE

Six Murders, Six Hangings

*　　*　　*

Chapter Twelve
'The means by which...'

The wealth of Britain attained through the Industrial Revolution was regarded with a mixture of admiration and envy in foreign fields, yet this prosperity resided with the few, for many poverty remained their daily diet. The divide between the poor and the better off became evermore pronounced and no one coined a better description of this than Benjamin Disraeli, when he used the term 'two nations'. In literature as in life, authors stayed within their known social stratas. Thus the novels of Jane Austen and the Brontës were concerned with a privileged society; neither Mr D'Arcy or Captain Wentworth ever came into contact with those who inhabited the lower classes. By contrast, with Dickens it is just as unbelievable to have the venerable Fagin or Bill Sykes conversing with Miss Elizabeth Bennett!

The poor however had one common denominator with the rich - exclusivity. The social structure of Victorian Britain was well-set, few if any brooking the divide between the different classes. Those of a working class background never became involved in the highways of public life. Oddly enough this engendered few complaints, they accepted their plight; overwhelming poverty, poor accommodation, frugality of existence, the constant battle with disease, intermittent employment and a shortened life expectancy.

There was a kind of resigned and weary acceptance of all of this, as if it was their 'lot' to be so brutalised. Their reward was to be found in the hereafter, for had not God created them so; this earthly struggle against their fate would raise them to a higher level, thus the chapel became the focal point where this would be constantly reaffirmed. They were already in the 'shadow of the valley of death' so redemption would automatically follow. Besides these essentially honest but poor people, there existed a lower class courted by vagabonds, thieves and murderers - the criminal layer.

As we have seen in Part One of this book, the Houses of Correction and the newly built prisons were littered with them. Many of those incarcerated had committed crimes that to modern eyes seem slightly ludicrous; gambling in the streets, hawking their wares, singing in public. The female prisoners were often prostitutes and were regulars to these institutions, although in Monmouthshire there has never been in Victorian times a case of a murderess being arraigned and convicted. Though the majority of the offences were of a minor nature, on rare occasions that most serious of crimes, murder, was brought before the courts.

Thus all the convictions and subsequent hangings carried out at Usk prison were of male prisoners, the victims with only one exception being female. What is most striking is the uniformity of the methods used to carry out these killings. Ironically the very class-consciousness of the Victorians proved to be a determining factor when it came to the choice of 'weapons'. The use of poison, the most insiduous and cold blooded of methods, required a visit to the local chemist. There you would have had to sign the Poisons Register, and more importantly convince the pharmacist that you had a bona fide reason for making the purchase - and murder was not one of them!

The use of poison was therefore the 'tipple' of the better off in society. The most infamous of poisoners included the Florentine family of the Borgias, whilst in Victorian times the medical profession tended to occupy such headlines. Dr Henry Lamson, a GP who through his addiction to morphine and the love of the good life often found himself in considerable debt. He had married into a rich family but the money was tied up with his wife's immediate relatives, especially her youngest brother Percy. So Lamson came to the 'reasonable' conclusion that if he could remove the said person, more money would become available. To that end the good doctor thoughtfully inpregnated a Dundee cake with aconite and presented it to the young man, who within hours of ingesting it died an agonising and protracted death. However by good police work Lamson was arrested, tried and convicted, ending his life on the scaffold on 18th April 1882.

Dr William Pritchard, a much-respected physician cold-bloodily poisoned with antimony both his wife and mother-in-law in the spring of 1865 when in pursuit of a younger woman. He too was eventually to come face to face with the hangman, but historically he was also the last person to be hanged in public in Scotland. A crowd estimated at around 100,000 witnessed his death. Dr Neil Cream many years later poisoned numerous women merely for the pleasure of it, apparently without any material gain. Of course the lower classes did sometimes use poison, but it was generally weedkiller and not the pure substances, although it was no less a potent killer.

The obstacle to obtaining a gun was that of money, no money no gun. Those without such means had to recourse to more 'homely' means, utilising what was freely available. Thus many of the murders carried out by those who inhabited the poorer classes were shocking in their brutality, in the very crudeness of the killings. Part One of this book attempted to illustrate the unremitting harshness of life behind prison walls, yet for many people the world outside was only marginally better.

The newly created pollution by the smoke-belching factories that the Revolution gave birth to, together with the vast slums of the large cities, orchestrated a contemporary version of Dante's *Inferno*! Even for those who found employment, life was generally hard, survival was a constant struggle. The manure that was randomly strewn on the streets by horses pulling carriages or hansoms, although unpleasant in the extreme, gave work to many a poor labourer. Keeping the streets clear of the endless flow of rubbish was also a job to be grateful for. Poverty was indeed incumbent to the system, it reigned supreme so when the matter of committing murder arose a basic but effective means was found.

The *knife*. In all its forms, from a simple piece of culinary equipment, to a razor, to a heavy-duty blade and axe. It was the weapon of choice. For this piece of glittering steel was gratefully employed by those wishing to take the lives of their fellow human beings. It had the advantage of being easily carried, easily hidden and after the deed was done, easily disposed of. The knife's great property was of course its effectiveness, as few survived a slash to the throat or a penetrating wound. As with the Llangibby murders previously described, the knife also triumphs in the following six cases. However in one unique episode the victim survived long enough to face her killer in court!

So the stage is set, the victims innocently come forward, their assailants more reluctantly for their deeds will eventually come to the notice of the one person they fear above all others, the hangman. His is the last eyes they will gaze into before they meet their Maker. Here then are their stories, the last six to die on the scaffold at Usk.

Chapter Thirteen
James Henry Gibbs 1874
What the butler didn't see...

When in pursuit of the ladies an easy charm if slightly obsequious manner was part of the armoury of James Gibbs. Born in Surrey, his advances were warmly if tragically welcomed by Jersey-born Ann Ingram who subsequently married him in July 1873 at St Helier. Almost immediately Gibbs brought his bride back to Cardiff as he was then employed as a butler to George Williams Esq. at Llanrumney Hall.

Like many a feckless husband before him, marriage did not interfere with his predatory instincts and within a short time he was seeing another woman who resided at nearby St Mellons. In fact Gibbs became infatuated with her but there was one major obstacle, the fetters of the marriage bonds. After much thought he conceived a plan, he must kill his wife, a plan he carried out on 12th May 1874. As a subterfuge he asked her to meet up with him so that they could discuss the marital problems they were both experiencing. On that fateful day he walked her to the edge of a farm owned by Samuel West and there viciously cut her throat, throwing the bloodied corpse into a nearby ditch.

Ann Gibbs was duly reported missing but an extensive search by police through St Mellons, Newport and Cardiff proved fruitless. Gibbs himself continued to carry out his duties at Llanrumney Hall with constant visits to the police to see if any progress had been made. On 3rd June, some three weeks after her murder, farmer Samuel West and his granddaughter were strolling around the outer fields of his land when they were attracted to the ditch in which she lay by the odour of rotting flesh. The body was badly decomposed with huge numbers of maggots still active.

When the police arrived they found that a watch engraved with her name still encircled her wrist; they also knew that James Gibbs wore a similar watch. In their enquiries the police had become more and more suspicious of him, so a decision was therefore made to keep the area under surveillance to see if he would attempt to revisit the scene of the crime. Sure enough, during night duty they saw a figure of a man approaching the ditch and on apprehending him they discovered the very person they were looking for - James Gibbs. He was immediately arrested and charged with the murder of his wife.

Gibbs was tried and found guilty on 6th August 1874 at Monmouth Assizes, the judge Mr Justice Lush donning the 'black' cap and pronouncing the sentence of death. He was immediately transferred to Usk Prison to await execution. Usk

Shire Hall, Monmouth Assizes.

Mr. Justice Lush.

being a small town, the news of Gibbs' detention and forthcoming execution had a profoundly depressing effect both on the local population and on the prison itself. This was to be the first private hanging there, the date of execution being fixed for Monday 24th August.

On the Sunday before there were numerous exhaltations and sermons from the pulpits of the various churches in and around Usk. In view of what was about to take place the following morning the Rev Steven Cattley Baker, vicar of St Mary's Anglican church gave as his reading, to his slightly awe stricken congregation, a text taken from Isaiah Chapter 5, verse 18:

> *'Woe unto them that draw iniquity with cords of vanity, and sin as it were with a cart rope...'*

There were contradictory reports of the state of Gibbs during his eighteen days in the condemned cell. *The Pontypool Free Press* merely stated that he had ate and drank heavily and slept well, however the *Star of Gwent* printed a totally different account by friends of the prisoner who had visited him in his cell. They stated that he intends if possible to destroy himself, so that he is being kept under the strictest surveillance, although they insist that on one occasion he tried to hang himself with strips of sheets off his bed and on another he tried to fatally injure himself by dashing his head against the stone walls of his cell. Both papers agreed however that on the Sunday night, his penultimate day on earth, he was understandably restless and uneasy. In accordance with his duties the governor of the prison Colonel Millman went to see him at 5 o'clock in the morning. He was still asleep but on being awoken Gibbs asked if the two warders in attendance could leave the cell so that he might be alone with the governor. Millman then asked him if he had anything to say.

'Yes. All I have to say is that I am innocent.'

The governor replied, *'The verdict of all the world is against you.'*

Gibbs stolidly insisted, *'I am innocent.'*

The governor then left but at 6.30am the Rev Cadwallader, Chaplain to the prison entered the cell and prayed with the prisoner for half an hour. Gibbs was then given his breakfast and on finishing the meal he was taken from the cell to meet William Marwood the public hangman, who immediately pinioned his arms. A little later the High Sheriff Mr Crawshay Bailey together with the Under Sheriff entered the prison. By then a small crowd of people had gathered outside with further groups at the corners of the streets of Usk. Meantime Dr James Boulton, Rev Cadwallder and Captain Herbert had entered the Magistrates Room, the window of which allowed a view of the excecution area.

When Marwood had inspected the scaffold assembly the previous day he found that there was insufficient length of drop for the execution, so he ordered that a hole should be dug to a depth of three feet beneath the scaffold and then painted black. At a few minutes before 8 o'clock on that Monday morning the Sheriff, the Under Sheriff and the Crier for the Sessions Mr Graham entered the condemned cell and in the presence of the prisoner the Chaplain began the service of the dead.

For some time previous Gibbs had been sobbing bitterly but at the commencement of the service he began to cry aloud. His cries echoed

Condemned man being exhalted by Chaplain to confess his guilt.

throughout the silent prison, echoed in the cells where the prisoners sat in awe, echoed in the corridors as the warders paced uneasily to and fro. In mortal fear Gibbs began to writhe in his chair to such an extent that Chief Warder Parker and his deputy Honess were forced to physically restrain him. Still struggling they moved slowly out of the room along the passage and on to the scaffold, with the Chaplain intoning *'I am the resurrection and the life…'*

By now Gibbs was in a near state of collapse as he was carried on to the platform of the scaffold where his agonised cries drowned out the recitation of the Chaplain. He was then asked if he had any final words, to which he sobbed:

'God forgive my sins. He knows I am innocent and am happy He knows I die innocent. Goodbye my parents, goodbye all. May the Lord have Mercy upon me.'

Marwood quickly placed the hood over his head and adjusted the noose around his neck and Gibbs was left alone over the trap door, still groaning, his entire frame trembling. As the Lord's Prayer was uttered Marwood pulled the lever and the struggles and life of James Henry Gibbs were over. It later transpired that his father had sent him a letter on the previous Saturday begging him to confess his guilt. He never did.

LINES ON THE

EXECUTION
OF
JAMES HENRY GIBBS,
Who was tried at the last Monmouth Assizes, and Sentenced to Death, for the MURDER of his WIFE at St. Mellons, near Cardiff, and Executed at Usk, August 24th. 1874.

London :- H.P.SUCH, Machine Printer and Publisher, 177, Union street, Borough.

Air-'Just before the Battle, Mother.'

The St. Mellons tragedy is ended,
  The murderer now has met his fate,
No one can escape God's justice,
  It must come either soon or late.
James Henry Gibbs upon the gallows,
  Met a most disgraceful doom,
Now his body it is lying,
  Decaying in the prison tomb.

CHORUS
Farewell! Father; farewell! Mother,
  When standing on the drop, he said,
Altho' I die upon the gallows,
  Oh, pray for me when I am dead.

We know is crime was so unmanly,
  That no pity could be shown,
The wife he should have loved and
  cherished,

That he murdered her is too well
  known;
He decoyed her to that little village,
  On that lovely summer's day,
And there 'twas in an ominous manner,
  That he took her life away.

When his victim she was missing,
  Search was made for her straightway,
Beneath the bushes, near St. Mellons,
  Her decaying body lay:
They found her - the sight was dreadful,
  For weeks her body had been there.
When the murderer was told of it,
  'I am innocent,' he did declare.

Many things was found upon him,
  That had belonged unto his wife,
It was plain that no one but him,
  Could have taken her dear life;
And when he was asked about her,
  'I am not married,' he did say,
He so untruthfully did answer,
  That himself he did betray.

Chapter Fourteen
Thomas Edwards 1892
Madness of a moment...?

The renowned market town of Abergavenny has been heralded as the 'gateway to Wales' with its juxtaposition to the Brecon Beacons and the Welsh hinterland. Perhaps it wasn't quite so ostentatiously described in Victorian times but it certainly came to the attention of a wider audience in the early 1890s when a particularly brutal murder took place there.

Daylight had quickly been waning when at about 9pm on the night of 16th September 1892 Edward Wilkins was returning home after an evening stroll. He was a railway guard with the London & North Western Railway Company so was hurrying back as he had an early start the following morning. As he approached the end of Hatherleigh Street near the junction with the Brecon and Merthyr Roads, he heard what sounded like heavy breathing coming from the rear of the Union Workhouse.

It was a somewhat isolated area in those days, an open field owned by a Mr Johnson having been recently converted into allotments with a partially completed new road running through it. Wilkins cautiously neared the place where the sound was coming from only to see the incumbent figure of a woman lying on her back in a pool of dark blood gasping for air. On closer inspection he was shocked to see that the blood was pouring from a deep gash across her throat.

In a state of panic Wilkins ran for help. This came in the form of PC Powell who was out on his beat when Wilkins almost ran into him. Both immediately returned to the scene of the crime where the police officer found the woman to be dead. He then contacted the station so that within a short period of time Superintendent Freeman and Dr Elmes Steel arrived. The body was still warm, lying face up in the gutter with her left arm extended and her right by her side. Blood and dirt besmirched her face and hands whilst her dress was pulled up to the knees. The doctor estimated that she had been attacked not more than an hour before.

Her body was then transferred to the mortuary where an autopsy was carried out. This revealed that the gash across her throat had been so deep that it had severed the windpipe and all the tissues in front of the vertebra including the ligaments and lining membrane of the bone itself. The left jugular was cut and this was to be reported as the cause of death. The doctor stated that a wound of such severity could only have been inflicted by the use of a very sharp knife and was definitely not suicide.

The murdered woman was soon identified as Mary Connolly the only daughter of 'Jerry' Connolly of 3 Pant-Lane Abergavenny. She was 24 years of age and single, but was well known to the local police and magistrates having been convicted on numerous occasions for prostitution, drunkeness and disorderly conduct.

Early the following morning the police began an intensive search of the area and found traces of blood on the barbed wire fence and also on the gate that led into the allotments. Within these allotments was a shed that was used to store various gardening implements and on the surrounding area they found bloodied footprints of two types, one small and one much larger. There were also spatters of blood on the cabbage patch adjacent to the shed. This obviously was the scene of the attack and the subsequent struggle. Their searches also turned up a lady's hat lying halfway between the shed and the fence. Later on the Saturday afternoon the police searches were considerably hampered by the rather ghoulish arrivals of hundreds of sightseers. Bad news always travels fast and many of those in the gathering crowds had travelled considerable distances, once more endorsing the old maxim of the attraction of the ugly!

Witnesses were not slow in coming forward. John Wyatt, a plasterer living in a street opposite Pant-Lane stated that he saw Mary Connolly talking to a man on the evening she was murdered. He described the man as being in his late twenties dressed respectably in dark clothes and wearing a hard hat. A Mrs Wilks also saw this man and besides her description closely matching that of John Wyatt she added that the stranger was a 'slingy' sort of fellow.

Given this and a certain amount of circumstantial evidence Sergeant Davies thought fit to arrest a William Saunders in Abergavenny on the Saturday evening. Under interrogation Saunders admitted to being with Mary Connolly on the Friday afternoon but had left her soon after. He had in fact aroused suspicion by the fact that between the fateful Friday night and the time of his arrest the next day he had on a different suit of clothes and unusually for him, had shaved. However to the consternation of the police Saunders managed to produce a cast iron alibi for the period in question.

A case in which the investigation had promised an early conviction looked almost certain was now thrown into a state of disarray. However the silver lining came at precisely 5pm on the Sunday when a man by the name of Thomas Edwards walked calmly into Abergavenny police station and announced to the duty sergeant that he wished to confess to the murder of Mary Connolly. Edwards a stout ex-army man of medium height was not a local man but knew Abergavenny well enough. In his discussions with the police he said that he had used an open razor on the deceased and offered to take them to the place where he had hidden it. So with Sergeant Capper and other officers in attendance he took them to a wall bordering a field adjacent to the allotments. There hidden from view lay the bloodied razor later shown to have mammalian blood adhering to its blade.

The coroner's inquest into the murder was conducted in the boardroom of the Union Workhouse before Mr J B Walford and a jury of thirteen men. They firstly were taken to view the body of the deceased which lay in another part of the workhouse. When this unpleasant duty had been performed they returned to the boardroom where they heard evidence from a series of witnesses including Superintendent Freeman, John 'Jerry' Connolly, Dr Elmes Steel and others relative to the case. The coroner eventually adjourned the inquest until the following Monday.

After spending a period of time on remand in Usk Prison, Edwards was committed for trial on 1st December 1892 at Monmouth Assizes before Mr Justice J C Day, with Mr A J Ram and Mr Rowlett appearing for the Crown whilst Mr T Corner represented Thomas Edwards. The prisoner was charged that he, 'on the 16th September 1892 in the parish of Abergavenny did feloniously, wilfully and of his malice aforethought, kill and murder Mary Connolly.'

To these charges the prisoner replied almost absentmindedly, 'Not guilty.' Many observers commented later on the odd behaviour of Edwards, as during the proceedings he appeared to have an apparent vacancy of expression as he gazed continually around the courtroom. The case for the prosecution was of course fairly straightforwad as they demonstrated through a number of witnesses that the prisoner had been drinking heavily throughout the Saturday in question. The prosecution carefully circumvented the true nature of the murdered woman by referring to her as 'an unfortunate creature, a woman of the town.'

They were also able to relate with some clarity the final hours in the life of the 'unfortunate creature.' Edwards and her had been seen to walk together down

Union Lane before turning up into Merthyr Road where they went into a pub, The Somerset Inn. Witnesses further testified to seeing them leave the inn and head towards the scene of the crime. The police and forensic evidence demonstrated that the murder had taken place at the allotments shed, and when Edwards left her lying there she managed with extraordinary willpower to crawl across a cabbage patch, through the wire fence only to finally collapse in the gutter where she was found by Edward Wilkins.

It would seem that in the face of such overwhelming evidence the defence counsel would have an almost impossible task, but whilst readily admitting that his client had indeed killed Mary Connolly, he argued that in reality Thomas Edwards was insane. To support this he proceeded to describe in detail the family background of his client. Edwards' mother had been declared insane and had spent many years within the local asylum. His grandfather was known locally as 'Silly Billy' whilst his uncle had been an imbecile who died when only fourteen years of age. The mere fact that his client had come to the police station to declare his guilt in the matter was further evidence of his abnormal state of mind.

When Mr Corner eventually put Edwards on the stand the accused stated in an unemotional voice that he had served in Egypt with the army but had developed pains in his head so that in 1888 he was invalided out with a very good character reference. He then continued by explaining that seven years ago his commanding officer Colonel Findal had been murdered in Birmingham by a 'loose' woman. Edwards then added:

> 'Since then I have always been against those girls. If I'd had a good chance
> I should have killed more!'

In direct rebuttal to this plea of insanity the prosecution called firstly Dr Glindinning the medical superintendent at Abergavenny Asylum. He told the court that he had visited the prisoner three times in the last month and had held long conversations with him. He had come to the firm conclusion that Edwards was of sound mind. Dr Donald Boulton medical officer to Usk prison said that he had also seen the prisoner on a daily basis and found no peculiarities. The last witness called for the Crown, Lieut. Colonel Surgeon Nelson stated that the prisoner's medical record whilst in the army showed no indication of mental illness.

After the judge's summing up the jury retired to consider their verdict but after a lapse of only ten minutes they returned to find the prisoner guilty. A deathly hush now settled on the court as Mr Justice Day, a person of much humanity, assumed the black cap and said with obvious emotion:

> 'Thomas Edwards, you have been found guilty on the clearest evidence, of
> the crime of wilful murder. Every effort has been made by counsel on
> your behalf to set up that at the time you committed this act you were of
> insane mind, and consequently no longer responsible for your act; but
> the evidence in support of that defence is utterly insufficient. No reasonable
> person could have come to any conclusion upon the evidence but that you
> took the life of that unhappy woman, being thoroughly conscious when
> you were killing her that you were doing wrong in so killing her. I never,
> upon occasions of this description, make any observations in reference to
> the particulars of the offence which has been committed. I should be sorry
> now if I were to harry your feelings by detaining you longer than the law
> makes it necessary. In addressing you now I would only beg one thing,
> and that I would beg of you, not as your judge, but I beg of you as your

fellow-man. Do pray take advantage, earnest advantage, of the time, for short though it be, it is abundantly sufficient to prepare yourself for meeting your God. The law in its mercy gives you time, which you unhappily did not give the poor creature who was your victim. You will have time, abundantly sufficient, to prepare yourself for the great change which awaits you.'

The judge then formally intoned the traditional words of the death sentence. During this speech Edwards remained apparently unconcerned, at the end of which he was led away and immediately transferred to the condemned cell in Usk prison to await execution on 27th December 1892. On the day prior to this James Billington (see Part Four) one of a family of state hangmen arrived at the Usk to make his preparations for the next day.

Prisoner in condemned cell with wardens.

The question of Edwards' sanity and whether he should hang had been widely discussed none more so than in the pubs and inns of Usk. By the early hours of the morning of the execution crowds had already began to gather in front of the prison, whilst within both Billington and Edwards had slept well, the latter being awoken and dressed at 6am to receive the prison chaplain in his cell.

Just before 8am with the lone bell tolling its soulful dirge the condemned man was transferred to a cell adjacent to the excution shed where John Billington was already waiting to quickly pinion the prisoner's arms. In company with the authorised officials Thomas Edwards walked calmly through the door and on to the centre of the scaffold. Still unheeding of his predicament the white hood was placed over his head, the noose quickly positioned, before Billington sprang the trapdoor to bring the life of Thomas Edwards to an end. As per tradition a black flag with the word 'Justice' was then hoisted above the prison.

Unlike modern court proceedings, criminal trials in Victorian times were completed in almost indecent haste. Yet in this particular case the question as to whether Edwards was insane is I feel more complex than the physicians of his day believed. Certainly he knew what he was doing when he killed Mary Connolly, but did he at the time think he was actually doing wrong as by his own utterances to rid the world of 'loose' women was a creditable act. The Scales of Justice have been known to swing rather uneasily on certain occasions.

Chapter Fifteen
Jeremiah Callaghan 1902
'The green-eyed monster...'

The emotive epithet 'a broth of a boy' to describe an Irishman could never be applied to Jeremiah Callaghan, for he was a moody reticent individual carrying a permanent 'chip' on his shoulder. As he had served for a number of years in the cookhouse of the Army he had earned locally the nickname of 'Jerry Canteen'. He was by nature a lazy man more often than not out of work and none too keen to acquire it. His domestic situation was exacerbated by the fact that his lover Hannah Shea had borne him a son and three daughters. The lack of means to provide for them meant that whilst he lodged in the town of Tredegar, Hannah and her children were confined to the Bedwellty Union workhouse.

The 38 year old Hannah still met up with Callaghan mostly on weekends but it was this separation that began to pray on the mind of the Irishman to the extent that he came to believe that she was seeing another man. His brooding nature soon allowed this to become more and more dominant in his thoughts as the days and weeks passed. He also decided that she was continually frittering away what little means they had on drink.

Saturday 4th October 1902 came around and Hannah with her children and friends from the workhouse walked slowly towards Tredegar. At this time Callaghan had actually taken a job as a labourer at a local stonemasons. When Hannah eventually arrived in Tredegar she sent her son who was now fourteen, to see a Mr Phillips the district relieving officer to obtain a promisary note that she needed in order to allow her to return to the workhouse that night.

The young lad whose name was also Jeremiah quickly found Mr Phillips, obtained the note and

Old Tredegar.

began the return journey to his mother at the town's railway station. His route took him past Morgan's yard where his father was employed. He found him in the store area and after a brief talk both left together and headed for the station. They arrived to find that Hannah and the children were not there so an irate Callaghan began to drag his son around the numerous pubs that existed in the town. At the Red Lion Inn a Mrs Price and her companion Mary Clifford told him that Hannah had gone to get a workhouse note from Mr Phillips. This didn't make any sense to the Irishman as his son had already got the required note.

Muttering oaths under his breath he quickened his pace along Commercial Road until he reached the Miners Inn. There he suddenly came upon Hannah who was sitting outside with her children and a Mrs Prothero. By now he was in a foul mood and accused Hannah of wasting good money on drink. When she hotly denied this he flew into an uncontrollable rage and knocked her to the ground. Regaining her feet she grabbed her son by the arm and purposefully marched away up Church Street closely followed by Callaghan. Luckily a policeman came into view so she breathlessly explained to him what had happened. After being warned about his behaviour Callaghan walked away so Hannah and her son returned to Mrs Prothero at the Miners Inn.

There now seemed to be a problem with the workhouse note that Hannah's son had given her so the three of them decided to go back to see Mr Phillips. They crossed Commercial Street but on entering The Circle they again came face to face with Callaghan. However he was by now contrite about the earlier events so they at last decided to make up by going to The Black Prince where he willingly paid for each round of drinks. When they left to go to the station they were both fairly intoxicated to the extent that opposite the market Callaghan stumbled and fell and only regained his feet with the help of Hannah.

With all three children around them the party set off down the path that led back to the workhouse. Stumbling and swaying Callaghan continued to fall over but with Hannah's help they slowly made their way down the narrow path. They must have appeared a rather incongruous procession with Jeremiah and two of his sisters in front then Callaghan and Hannah and finally bringing up the rear the third sister. As they reached roughly the midpoint of their journey they met Jane Hannam, a friend who also resided at the workhouse. As she and Hannah began to chat nobody noticed the change that was taking place in Jeremiah Callaghan.

The alcohol-fuelled turmoil in his brain had slowly fermented into an uncontrollable rage, the fateful moment had arrived for Hannah Shea. He thrust his hand in his pocket and withdrew something that glinted menacingly in the afternoon sun - a knife. Uttering a cry like a wild animal he pushed Hannah against a nearby wall and viciously drew the sharp blade across her throat. With an agonising scream she managed to squirm free from his grasp and run as fast as possible down the hill. Crying with anger and shock young Jeremiah starting throwing stones at his father but when Callaghan still brandishing the knife turned in his direction son and daughters fled in terror up the hill.

Hannah who had gone in the opposite direction had miraculously reached the bottom before collapsing. Sarah Morris, a cleaner at the workhouse who was standing talking on the hillside with her boyfriend heard the screams and hurried towards the stricken woman. They passed both Callaghan leaning drunkenly against the wall and the fleeing children before they got to Hannah. Sarah Morris went down on her knees and cradled the dying woman in her lap as blood oozed from the terrible wound at her throat. William Pritchard a local collier now arrived on the scene and immediately took Sarah's apron and wrapped it tightly about Hannah's throat in an attempt to staunch the flow of blood.

Next came the welcome form of Amy Pearl a district nurse who after quickly assessing Hannah's condition hurried away to fetch her first-aid kit. Callaghan himself had by now managed to stagger to the workhouse where he was seen by the nurse as she was about to go by. She hesitated and then went into the office of William Thomas the master of the workhouse and told him about what had just happened, whereupon he summoned Callaghan to come and see him immediately.

Callaghan appeared quite calm and totally unaffected by the situation although Thomas noticed that the Irishman's hands were heavily bloodstained as were the sleeves of his coat. Back at the hillside Hannah Shea was fighting for her life as her friends were still vainly trying to stop the blood flow. After a few more dreadful minutes Hannah's breathing became shallower until it ceased altogether and death overtook her. The sad little group now picked up her lifeless form and gently carried her to the workhouse mortuary. On being made aware of this William Thomas informed Callaghan of his lover's death whereupon he asked to see his children. Thomas replied 'Not just now' as he awaited the arrival of the police. Callaghan then stumbled out into the workhouse yard where to the amazement of everyone he began to jig and dance as if he didn't have a worry in the world!

On the arrival of the police he was taken into custody but unable to speak coherently he was left until the next day to sober up. On being then informed of his arrest Callaghan professed to having no knowledge of attacking Hannah Shea being totally surprised when informed of her death. He next made a brief appearance on Monday 6th October at Tredegar police court where he was remanded in custody until the forthcoming inquest. His only comment was that he wished to see his children but this was denied as they were now back at the workhouse.

The inquest that took place on 7th October 1902 before James Berry Walford was really only a formality and the jury took a matter of a few minutes to find him guilty of wilful murder and convict him to trial on the Coroner's warrant. Further hearings took place on 13th and 21st October when after witnesses had given evidence Callaghan was committed for trial at the next assizes. This took place at Monmouth on 22nd November 1902 before Mr Justice Forbes, with Mr JRV Marchant KC leading for the Crown and Mr H Hardy KC for the defence.

The various witnesses were once more assembled and reiterated what they had seen or knew about the killing of Hannah Shea. A Mr John Williams an engine driver of 49 Whitworth Street Tredegar added that he saw Callaghan picking up bits of paper off the ground of the hillside and attempting to use them to wipe blood off his hands. William Pritchard entered the witness box to state that at about 6.20pm on the day of the murder he had seen Callaghan, Hannah and the children near Lewis Price's shop in Tredegar. Callaghan appeared to be so drunk that Hannah had to support him but even so he still fell down in the gutter.

Nurse Amy Pearl who had attended to the stricken woman in her final moments said that when the body was transferred to the workhouse she found that the dead woman's purse contained only a few halfpenny coins. On closer examination she then noticed that under the congealed blood on Hannah's left hand was a scrap of paper which when cleaned proved to be part of the relieving officer's admission order to enable the family to be allowed into the workhouse that night. The nurse's lips quivered with undisguised emotion as she relayed this to the silent court.

One of the chief witnesses for the prosecution was the GP/surgeon Dr Isaac Crawford who had arrived on the hillside at around 6.35pm. At that time Hannah Shea was still alive but on examination he quickly realised that her chances of survival were extremely slim as she had a deeply incised wound on the left side of her neck. Despite the best efforts of himself and Nurse Pearl the massive blood loss soon took its toll and Hannah died at 6.45pm just as the ambulance was arriving.

The following day Dr Crawford performed a post mortem on the dead woman which revealed the full savagery of the knife attack for in addition to the jugular being severed, two other main arteries had been cut by the force used by Callaghan. He also discovered a injury to the head which was probably caused when Callaghan struck her earlier in the afternoon. The doctor also went to the workhouse to examine Callaghan himself where he found him to be in an intoxicated condition although able to converse in slurred tones.

The final witness for the prosecution was Superintendent Francis Allen who had been informed by John Williams of the incident on the hill near the workhouse. He immediately went to the scene arriving just as Hannah passed away, so leaving the doctor and nurse with the body he continued down the path to the workhouse. There he saw Callaghan in the yard with other workhouse men, walking around calmly smoking his pipe. Allen quietly took him by the arm and led him into the building where he cautioned him before charging him with murder.

The police officer then began a search of Callaghan and immediately found a knife, still wet with blood, in his left waistcoat pocket. Further searching revealed an empty Irish whiskey bottle and 6 shillings in loose change. Superintendent Allen also told the court that the backs of Callaghan's hands were spattered with blood. The next day he conducted a search of the hillside retracing Hannah's last journey where he soon discovered the missing fragment of the workhouse admission ticket which matched that found on the dead woman.

Faced with such overwhelming evidence against his client, Mr Hardy could only put forward a plea of insanity. He suggested that Callaghan's action was a momentary outburst of insane propensity resulting from an attack of *delirium tremens*. This was in contradiction to the earlier evidence given by Dr D Boulton, surgeon to Usk prison, who after a careful examination of the prisoner found no such mental condition existed.

In his closing speech to the jury the defence counsel eloquently argued that there was no intention of committing such a crime, quoting a precedent in *R. v Cox* which stated, 'If delirium tremens caused a degree of madness, even if only temporary, it relieved a prisoner from criminal responsibility ...' After the judge gave direction on various points of law to the jury they retired to consider their verdict. Callaghan's behaviour throughout the trial was curious in the extreme as either he was gazing almost absentmindedly around the court or he was chatting affably with his solicitor.

Ominously the jury returned within the space of 35 minutes and on being asked for their decision they delivered a 'guilty as charged' verdict. Mr Justice Forbes then donned the black cap and to a subdued court passed the death sentence on the prisoner. Before Callaghan was taken away the judge offered the following warning, 'I don't wish by any words of mine to aggravate the painful situation in which you stand, but from the circumstances under which you committed murder, I can hold out to you no hope of reprieve.'

The date of execution was set for Friday 12th December 1902, and the learned judge's opinion was validated when on 10th December Callaghan was told that his appeal had been turned down. The day before the execution the public hangman and his assistant William and John Billington [*see* Section Four] arrived at Usk prison to make their preparations. Friday dawned to a bleak cold morning as if in sympathy with the grim business at hand. The condemned man had had a fitful sleep that night but without much delay eventually stood on the chalked T on the boards of the scaffold. A priest lifted a crucifix to his lips as Callaghan cried out in a husky voice, 'Holy Mother pray for me!. Jesu help me!' Seconds later he was hanging limp at the end of the rope.

Chapter Sixteen

John Edmunds 1909
'A note for the hangman...?'

The Eastern valley town of Abersychan is cradled between the giant pillars of Pontypool in the south and Blaenavon in the north and whilst its former glories in the iron and coal industries are now distant memories, one 'industry' remains still, that of sheep farming on the precipitous hillsides that surround the town. These farm holdings were carefully distanced from each other to enable each to be viable and provide a livelihood for the men and women who spent their lives working them. By their very nature they exist in isolation, and this provided the perfect backdrop to a cruel, sustained and savage attack during the first decade of the twentieth century. As will be seen the subsequent legal proceedings were somewhat unusual in that the victim was able to give evidence against the perpetrator in an actual murder trial!

Unlike modern times valley children in the Edwardian era were generally quite safe from molestation or abduction, so there was nothing unusual for 11 year old Percy Evans and his younger sister Kathleen to take a walk from their home at Nant-y-Maelor across the mountainside to visit a neighbour on a cold Saturday afternoon in February 1909. The purpose of the journey was simply to deliver a newspaper to 59 years old Cecilia Harris who lived at and managed Garnwen Farm near Abersychan.

Garnwen Farm.

The recently whitewashed farmhouse lay within a hollow on the side of Lasgarn mountain surrounded on all sides by a broad expanse of meadowland. Adjacent to the southern side of the house were haylofts and outbuildings, whilst in the front a solid walled porch led to the entrance. The approach to this farm was by means of a long winding rugged lane, rising steeply from Abersychan. It was of course a lonely place and a Mr H Rowlands the standing tenant had often advised Mrs Harris, without success, to reside in the town for her own safety.

The route that the two children took led them across the steep hillside, so it wasn't until around 4.00pm that they eventually arrived at the gate of the farm. On turning to close the gate they noticed for the first time that a man was standing on the mountain looking down at them. He was near enough for the children to see him quite plainly as he was wearing a dark suit and light cap with a stripe down it. More menacingly they also noticed that he carried a shotgun in the crook of his left arm. The two children turned away from him as Cecilia Harris greeted them from the door of the farmhouse. They all went inside and no doubt enjoyed a warm drink before leaving on their homeward journey at around 4.35pm.

On arriving back at Nant-y-Maelor they found that their parents still hadn't returned from a visit to Pontypool, so the younger sister Kathleen decided to return

Cecilia Harris murdered by John Edmunds, Abersychan.

to Garnwen Farm and wait there until she was collected by either her mother or father. By the time she got to Cecilia's the time was nearing half past five and the light was beginning to fade. As she undid the catch on the gate Kathleen heard a low moaning sound and on entering the farmyard she suddenly saw Cecilia Harris lurching towards her. It was a grotesque sight for the little girl as Cecilia's face, hands and dress were soaked with blood. Momentarily paralysed with fear Kathleen let out a scream and ran homewards.

By an extraordinary effort of willpower Cecilia now made the long journey to a neighbouring farm but on arriving there found it deserted. Courageously she set off to cover the half-mile to Penyrheol Farm, the next place of habitation. At the limits of her endurance she staggered against the farmhouse door, her desperate cries being overheard by the owner William Rees. On opening the door he involuntarily stepped back in horror at the appalling sight that met his eyes, then reacting quickly he and his wife Polly carried the collapsing woman inside and at the same time sent their daughter Eliza to Abersychan to fetch the doctor. Their initial shock had now turned to utter disbelief that a woman in this state could have managed to walk the distance between the two farms.

As they both attempted to staunch the flow of blood from the gash across her throat and from the jaw and head injuries, Cecilia desperately tried to croak out the name of her assailant. Eventually she whispered the name of John Edmunds also known as 'Jack the poacher'. Rees then gave Cecilia a piece of scrap paper and a pencil and on it she managed to scrawl the words: *'Jack Edmunds shot me and cut my throat he got my money. Cecilia Harris'*. This blood stained piece of paper was eventually passed to the police.

Dr McCormack now arrived at the farm and whilst waiting for the ambulance tended to the needs of Cecilia. A little later Superintendent James James and Sergeant Albert Jones also reached Penyrheol and after a brief discussion with the occupants they both left and made their way to Garnwen Farm. Shortly afterwards the

John Edmunds.

ambulance arrived and Cecilia Harris was taken down the valley to Pontypool District Hospital. As they made their way across the mountainside the two police officers must have experienced acute anxiety, for this case differed considerably from their normal diet of crime which usually revolved around drunks, thieving and the ever present domestic violence.

On reaching Garnwen they began taking detailed notes of the scene that met their eyes. There were bloodstains on the gate and on the ground leading to the door of the farm which was still open. They noted that the kitchen window was smashed in and glass strewn around the floor. There were further bloodstains on the door whilst the kitchen was also heavily contaminated and a closer examination revealed the knife that had been used on the unfortunate woman. A number of drawers had been opened and visibly ransacked.

As little else could be achieved that night the Superintendent secured the premises and then sent Sergeant Jones in search of John Edmunds. As he was well known to the police Jones knew that the suspect lived with his mother at 41 High Street Abersychan so a mere twenty minutes later he was knocking on the door of the house. The startled mother of Edmunds answered the door and told Jones that her son wasn't at home adding that she had no idea where he was or when he would return.

A next-door neighbour William Morgan told him that he had seen Edmunds at around 6.15pm washing his face and hands in the back kitchen. Rather suprisingly the sergeant now left saying that he would call again.

In fact he returned in the early hours of the following morning to find his suspect asleep in bed. He was immediately cautioned and then

High Street, Abersychan. John Edmunds was arrested at his home there.

arrested on suspicion of attempted murder before being taken to the local police station. A morose and taciturn man, Edmunds insisted that he was in nearby Garndiffaith all that day not returning home until 5.40pm when he sat down to tea with a little girl called Mary Taylor. He further stated that a friend William Morgan had called at the same time to see if he was going to the local theatre that night. Edmunds said that he had agreed to this and went with another friend Benjamin Hill and didn't return until well after 10pm.

Whilst the police began the process of checking the validity of his statements, they heard from the local hospital that Cecilia Harris although still critically ill had somehow survived her ordeal and was now conscious. Superintendent James now decided on a course of action which today would raise a few eyebrows; he had Edmunds taken to the hospital ward so that Cecilia could see him face to face, hopefully to make a positive identification of her attacker, which she did! Worried that she might not live much longer they also took a statement from her on the same evening.

John Edmunds was now charged with attempted murder to which he replied, *'I know nothing about it.'* He was kept in custody at the police station until the following morning when he was brought before the magistrates at Pontypool. The prisoner was represented by a local solicitor Harold Saunders, the brief appearance only to give evidence of arrest. A series of further remands took place in order to allow Cecilia Harris time to recover from her ordeal. The weeks went by with Edmunds being held in Usk Prison until the third week in April 1909 when the hospital doctors advised the police that she was now well enough to leave and give evidence.

On 23rd April she duly appeared in court where Mr Horace Lynne prosecuting, told the magistrates that in addition to attempted murder Edmunds would also be indicted for rape. With these two counts against him he was remanded for trial at the forthcoming assizes at Monmouth. Events now took a dramatic turn as Cecilia Harris suffered a deterioration in her condition, ultimately dying on Wednesday 5th May 1909. The charge against Edmunds was now changed from *attempted* murder to one of *wilful* murder.

The trial took place on 7th June under Mr Justice Ridley, with Mr Cranstoun KC leading for the Crown and Mr SRC Bosanquet KC for the defence. After one juror was challenged and subsequently replaced, the Crown opened proceedings by calling a series of witnesses to testify against Edmunds. His proximity to Garnwen Farm on the afternoon of Saturday 20th February when the attack took place was firmly established by a number of testimonies. A collier William Annetts explained that he was walking with his friend Joseph Jaynes through Lasgarn at 3.00pm on that day when they briefly met and spoke with Edmunds who on leaving them made off in the direction of Garnwen.

Albert Trumper a farmhand thought he had seen the accused who was wearing a dark suit and light cap, between 3.00 and 4.00pm near some rocks that overlooked Garnwen. Eleven years old Percy Evans had attended an identification parade on 22nd February and immediately picked out Edmunds as the man he had seen when he had visited Cecilia with his sister. William Rees who had taken in and helped the murdered woman also revealed that he too had seen Edmunds at around 4.00pm near Garnwen Farm and added that the accused was carrying a gun and staring intently at the farm.

Mark Williams a collier from Harpers Road, Talywain said that he saw Edmunds paying for fruit from a shop in the High Street at Abersychan with a five shilling piece. Another witness William Alonzo Roden a publican from Garndiffaith stated that the accused attempted to buy from him cartridges for his gun on 19th February, the day before the murder.

George Thompson a County Analyst, the precursor to today's forensic scientists, reported that he had found blood on the left breast and left sleeve of the coat Edmunds wore that day. The coat and a vest had various lengths of hair attached, whilst some greyish to golden brown eyelashes were also present. Seminal fluid had been isolated from two of the garments. Thompson had further determined that the blood on the knife used in the attack was of the same type as that of the deceased.

These witnesses conjured up between them an overwhelming weight of evidence for the prosecution, however the jury must have been even more shocked by the information supplied by Dr McCormack when he described the condition of Cecilia Harris on his examination of her at Penyrheol Farm. She was in shock due to excessive blood loss, having cuts on the palms of her hands probably due he thought to her attempts to defend herself. A bullet fired at close range had fractured her jaw and inflicted an elongated wound on the right side of her face running from behind her mouth down to the midline of the lower jaw. In addition she had suffered a four-inch long cut to her throat which had partially severed the windpipe.

Dr John Mulligan who was resident at Pontypool Hospital and had administered to her there also carried out the post mortem. His autopsy findings showed that death had been caused by heart failure due to congestion of the lungs. There were also signs of fatty degeneration, bronchitis and kidney disease. However Dr Mulligan categorically stated that notwithstanding these medical findings, he had no doubt that the injuries that were sustained by her in the attack were the eventual cause of her death.

The final and most damning witness was not actually present - being the victim herself! Cecilia Harris had left with the police her deposition dictated whilst she was in hospital, and it was this document that the Crown prosecutor now read to a subdued court who listened with increasing horror as the facts of that day were relentlessly unfolded. She began by stating that at around 5pm on 20th February she was working on the farm with Albert Trumper and Mr Rowlands' son, when she first noticed John Edmunds. He was standing on the mountainside about a hundred yards away and was cradling a gun in his arms.

Soon after Trumper and Rowlands left for home and after going indoors Cecilia brought out a bucket of ashes only to find Edmunds now standing in her garden. She told him to leave which he did but only as far as a hayrick adjacent to the garden, where he proceeded to smoke a cigarette. She shouted once more at him but his only reaction was to lift his gun and mockingly point it at her. Becoming slightly anxious she quickly retreated inside the house, making sure that the kitchen door was locked behind her. In order to see what Edmunds was up to Cecilia went upstairs and on looking out of the bedroom window she saw him put down his gun and climb over the garden wall. She next heard the sound of breaking glass coming from the kitchen as he forced his way in.

The now terrified woman ran back down the stairs and attempted to flee via the open front door but as she reached the garden gate she half turned to see Edmunds pick up his gun and fired, the bullet hitting her on the side of the face. Striding up to her he struck the helpless woman a savage blow knocking her to the ground whereupon he tore off her underclothes and raped her. This act was repeated as with his greater strength he managed to pinion her on her back.

After his lust was slated Cecilia attempted to calm him down and asked if her face was cut. He nodded so regaining her feet she staggered back to the kitchen to get water to bathe her wounds. As Edmunds followed her in, she in desperation told him to take whatever money she had if only he would leave at once. From a drawer in the dresser she gave him 5s 6d, which included a five-shilling piece. He now stood there seemingly unable to decide whether to go or not, when his attention was suddenly caught by the sight of a white-handled carving knife lying on the table. With one swift movement he grasped it, pulled the half feinting woman's head back by the hair and viciously cut her throat. In a maniacal rage Edmunds then grasped her head and repeatedly dashed it against the kitchen floor.

In the midst of this horrendous attack Cecilia Harris managed to gasp out, 'For the Lord's sake spare me! Think of your mother!' This agonising plea made him falter and he stepped back as if considering what to do. Cecilia now stumbled out through the door into the garden where at that very moment young Kathleen Evans arrived at the gate before the terrified child ran away home. Edmunds himself now came outside and with the heartless words, 'I can bugger off now anytime', he left Cecilia to her fate.

This deposition spoken quietly by the Crown advocate in the dry and dusty atmosphere of the courtroom stunned the listening jury as whitefaced they turned to gaze at the prisoner standing apparently unmoved in the dock. The defence team of course had no witnesses to call, but Mr Bosanquet did his best for his client by offering to the jury the testimony of the medical staff that Cecilia Harris had been certified as dying of general bronchitis, heart and kidney disease. Therefore he pointed out Edmunds could be found guilty of rape and assault, but not murder. The jury, after the Judge's summing up, retired to consider their verdict but returned in a very short time to find the prisoner guilty of murder.

Mr Justice Ridley after agreeing with this verdict now donned the black cap and pronounced the death sentence on John Edmunds. However the prisoner simply smiled around the court seemingly oblivious of the seriousness of his position and showed an apparent reluctance to 'go below'. He was then escorted to the railway station in Garndiffaith and locked in a central compartment with a number of police officers under the charge of Sergeant Jones. Many people from the area including Edmunds' mother and her two sisters travelled in the front compartments. On reaching Usk station a great crowd of people eagerly lined the platform to catch a last glimpse of the condemned man who continued to smile at all around him before being taken to the local prison.

An appeal against the capital charge was now made by Edmunds' counsel based on the claim that Cecilia Harris had died much later of a medical condition and not because of the attack. On 18th June the Appeal Judges headed by the Lord Chief Justice, Lord Alverston heard the case and after deliberation firmly turned down the appeal. Bosanquet now played his final card in an attempt to save the life of his client by appealing directly to the Secretary of State for clemency.

The execution date was now set for Saturday 3rd July so for the next three weeks Edmunds occupied the condemned cell at Usk prison with two warders in constant attention. He received visits from his mother and his family but otherwise seemed unpeturbed by the position he was in. On 30th June his fate was sealed when his solicitor received the following letter from the Home Office:

> *I am desired by the Secretary of State to inform you that he has given careful consideration to the petition forwarded by you on behalf of John Edmunds, now under sentence of death, and I am to express to you his regret that after consideration of the facts of the case, he fails to discover any sufficient grounds to justify His Majesty to interfere in the due course of the law.*
>
>

I am Sir, Yours obediently
E. Blackwell
>

On the day before the execution Henry Pierrepoint, the Hangman with his assistant John Ellis were received into Usk prison and set about their task of ensuring that the erected scaffold was in working order and that they had the opportunity to view the prisoner in order to calculate accurately the length of the desired drop. That night Edmunds slept fitfully but was on occasions heard to scream out in his sleep.

By a quarter to eight a crowd estimated at well over 200 had formed in the road and waste ground opposite the prison. Many were colliers who had travelled from the Eastern valleys, but amongst them also were a number of women. Some of the crowd were vying with each other to obtain the best vantage point in the hope of catching a glimpse of the scaffold. This of course was not possible.

Meanwhile as the hour of eight approached the prisoner was transferred from the condemned cell to another adjacent to the place of execution. At a few minutes to eight the prison Chaplain, the Rev. William Jones of Llansoy entered the cell followed by Pierrepoint who on asking the prisoner to stand and turn proceeded to pinion his arms behind his back. Edmunds held by two warders was then escorted on the short walk to the execution chamber by the Chaplain, Dr E. Hackett the prison medical officer, John Moxon the Under-Sheriff, the prison governor, and Pierrepoint and John Ellis. As he was led on to the scaffold Edmunds' legs began to sag and he murmured an inaudable comment.

However as the two warders reached out to give a steadying hand he recovered himself and managed a smile as the white hood was placed over his head and the noose adjusted around his neck. John Ellis the assisant hangman had already strapped his legs and as he threw himself off the trapdoors Edmunds gave a last moan before Pierrepoint pushed the lever sending the prisoner to an instantaneous death. Dr Hackett then descended into the pit and certified that life was extinct. In order to avoid the crowds still standing outside, Henry Pierrepoint and John Ellis left the prison by a door giving access to the Sessions House, then made their way across

Sessions House, Usk.

the fields to the Chepstow Road from where they were driven back to Usk station in time to catch the 10.05 train!

An odd postscript to this case came a few days after the hanging when a local newspaper, *The Free Press of Monmouthshire*, published the following letter from Mr G. Jones, the Manager of Woodfield Colliery Blackwood, who didn't realise until too late that he knew the executed man:

Court room at Sessions House, Usk. Tunnel led from Court to prison next door.

Sir - The account of the execution of John Edmunds at Usk on Saturday is gruesome reading, and the question arises naturally, 'Was the condemned man accountable for his actions?' The deed committed was so dastardly that I am afraid that the mental condition of Edmunds was not inquired into by the proper authorities as it should have been.

That his mind was at times unhinged I am certain, for near the end of February 1908 I dismissed him because of his strange actions, as I felt that it was not safe for him to work underground. He was employed as a night haulier.

For about a fortnight after he was dismissed and paid off he would hang around the colliery, and if he saw a tram of rubbish on the rubbish tip he would take a shovel, which he always carried with him, and discharge it, or do some other work if I was not about, the men of course allowing him. As soon, however, as he would see me coming he would get away. I found out that he would get into a disused level and would begin working without anybody knowing. I consequently had to threaten to send for the police before I got him to stay away. He would however not apply for any pay for the work he had done.

That he was not 'compos mentis' was quite evident, and that was the only reason I had for dismissing him.... On Saturday an insane man was led to the gallows, and although the crime that he committed was most revolting, the fact whether he was sane or insane, should have been properly inquired into....

Chapter Seventeen
William Butler 1909
'Revenge is a double-edged sword...'

As professional killers are few and far between it follows that practically all capital crimes are committed by rank amateurs. Thus the job of detection by the police is often helped by the amateurish methods employed by our hapless killers. This naturally does not preclude the existence of the 'perfect' crime as its very perfection would make it unknown and thus undetectable. The case of William Butler fortunately falls in the category of not only amateur but actually inept. The three elements that are normally associated with murders and murderers are lust, greed and hatred. What is unusual about this crime is that all three of these were present when Butler planned and carried out his killings. However our story begins not at the scene of the crime but in a neighbouring house, the home of the West family.

The Edwardian era often conjures up visions of extravagant house parties, long languid summer evenings, drowsily played cricket matches and the carefree adventures of the Grand Tour through Europe and the Far East. The reality for most of the population however was the daily struggle against poverty, where scrimping and saving were the only means of subsistence in old age. This was the situation that existed with the Mr and Mrs West, their 15 years old daughter Florence and her younger brother Frederick all living at Pye Corner, Newport. Florence was in service, but to help with the family budget Elizabeth West decided, with some misgivings, to take in a lodger.

So William Butler came to stay with them at a rent of 10s per week. He was sixty-two years old when he arrived and almost immediately took an unhealthy shine to young Florence but she firmly resisted his unwelcomed advances. This in turn caused him to be evermore fractious and abusive until Florence's parents decided that the situation could no longer be endured and told him to leave at once. This he did, but not before hurling a torrent of invectiveness and threats at the Wests and in particular Florence.

Butler now took up lodgings further along the street with a Mr and Mrs Doody and their son Sam aged eight. Yet his harrassment of Florence continued unabated; to such an extent that Mr West was forced to go to the police who promptly issued Butler with a summons. He appeared before the magistrates on 6th November 1909 and was bound over to keep the peace. Unfortunately this had little or no influence on his subsequent behaviour.

William Butler who killed Mary and Charlie Thomas at Tank Cottage.

Florence was employed as a servant to a John Ricketts the stationmaster at Bassaleg station, but as she journeyed to and fro from her home Butler constantly followed her. She would only reply 'good morning' or 'good night' to his entreatise to either marry him or to run away with him to North Wales. His manner gradually became more aggressive so Florence's parents often accompanied her home at night. However on the evening of 8th November she left alone and almost immediately he accosted her, but again she firmly rebuffed him. This time Butler flew into a rage and shouted at her, 'If you don't speak to me I will make you suffer for it!'

The young girl now took fright and quickly retraced her steps back to John Ricketts' house where she explained to him what had occurred. He decided that the best course was to call a policeman and as a result Butler received a second summons, though in the meantime he issued threats against Ricketts as well. On Friday 13th November he was again in front of the magistrates and this time was given a fine of £10 with additional court costs of 12s 6d. If these fines were not paid he would be sent to prison for 14 days. With the rage still upon him he decided to go to prison.

However that Friday was to prove an even more fateful day for Butler. It was just after eight o'clock in the morning when young Frederick West found a key lying on the kitchen windowsill of his house. He gave it to his mother who thought that it might belong to her sister who was a frequent visitor there. Frederick was therefore sent with the key to his aunt's but soon returned to say that it didn't belong to her. Elizabeth West shook her head in puzzlement but as she had to get on with her chores, the key was put on a shelf and dismissed from her thoughts.

It was some time later that Elizabeth realised that she hadn't seen any signs that day of her nearest neighbours Charlie and Mary Thomas who lived at Tank Cottage. Charlie was now 82 and had retired some three months before with an arthritic condition affecting his hands. Mary his wife was ten years younger than him and was known locally as a rather eccentric woman. Elizabeth's anxiety increased as the day wore on with still no sightings of the couple. As evening approached she decided to call on a friend living nearby, Alice Llewellyn, and together they made their way to Tank Cottage.

They knocked on the door but received no response and peering through the windows wasn't possible as the curtains were still drawn. Elizabeth then had an idea and quickly going back to her own house she retrieved the key that had mysteriously appeared on her windowsill. On inserting it into the doorlock of Tank Cottage it turned easily. Both women now cautiously entered the hallway and whilst Elizabeth called out to Mr and Mrs Thomas, Alice went into the kitchen. There she was dismayed to see the place in a shambles with cupboard drawers pulled out and their contents strewn on the floor. She went back to Elizabeth and after a whispered discussion they carefully locked the door behind them and left in order to find a policeman.

It was around seven o'clock when PC Thomas Baile arrived and by using the key that Elizabeth gave him he let himself into Tank Cottage. The house once more remained silent to his calls, so without waiting any longer he climbed the stone steps leading to the bedrooms. On opening the door to the main bedroom his worst fears were confirmed as he saw the elderly couple lying on the bed. However their sleep was the sleep of the dead. Charles Thomas lay on his back his head having been so severely battered that brain tissue was exposed. His wife Mary was lying on her side away from

Charlie and Mary Thomas killed by William Butler.

93

Police outside Tank Cottage.

him, but the blood-soaked blanket that covered her head left no doubt about her fate as well.

He carefully inspected the room taking care not to disturb anything which might provide a clue to the murderer. Baile noted that at the foot of the bed was a satchel containing an empty bloodstained purse. The bedclothes and parts of the floor were also heavily contaminated with blood as was some of the sparse furniture. After a cursory glance around the other rooms PC Baile descended the stairs and ushering the women out he informed them of what he had seen before sending them home. He then relocked the cottage and quickly made his way to a telephone to inform his superiors.

Within a matter of half an hour Inspector John Barry accompanied by a number of constables arrived to take charge of the case. The first piece of evidence he gathered was a small jacket smeared in manure which had obviously been used on the window next to the door in order to deaden the sound of breaking glass. On learning from Constable Baile that the key to the Tank Cottage door had been in the possession of Mrs West he immediately went to see her taking the jacket with him. To his surprise Elizabeth West instantly recognised it as belonging to her daughter Florence, a garment she had discarded months before. She also explained how her young son had come across the key and given it to her.

John Barry had not become an inspector for nothing and recognised that the West family was a basically decent hardworking family and unlikely to have committed such a barbaric crime. Naturally as the circumstantial evidence was pointing in their direction it was logical to assume that someone was deliberately carrying out a vendetta against them. He therefore asked Mrs West if she could think of anyone who would be likely to hold such a grudge and he listened with growing interest as she recited the non-stop tirade that William Butler had been waging against them and in particular Florence.

It was on the following morning, Saturday, that Butler once more appeared before the magistrates who this time sentenced him to fourteen days in prison. On being searched he was found to have £1 12s on him plus a glass-cutter's diamond. That same morning PC Baile visited Butler's lodgings at 3 Jones' Terrace, Pye Corner and took notes of his conversations with the landlords there, Robert and Cicely Doody. They told him that Butler had gone to bed at about quarter past seven on the Thursday evening and on rising at seven the next morning had left without having breakfast.

Robert Doody added that he had heard snoring during the night but was unsure as to whether it was Butler or his young son Samuel. He told Baile that his lodger next appeared at about 6.00pm on the Friday evening and told them that as he had eaten ham and eggs in Cardiff he wasn't hungry. It came as no surprise to the police officer to hear that since Butler had come to stay with them he had consistently avoided paying for his full board and lodgings.

The question of Butler's financial position now became pivotal to the police investigation. After returning from Cardiff on the Friday evening he had given

Cicely Moody six pennies and told her to buy some 'supper' beer. He also mentioned that he had been to see his solicitors with regard to his appearance before the magistrates on the Saturday morning. This prompted the police to visit the firm of Lloyd & Cross where a Mr Evan Davies confirmed that Butler had indeed called at about 2pm on the Friday. They had discussed his forthcoming summons for which Butler had paid a fee of two guineas in the form of one sovereign, two half sovereigns and a florin. Butler's ability to pay this sum was certainly at odds with his previous financial position.

Not only had he been unable to keep up with his weekly rent, he had also attempted on the Thursday to borrow five shillings from two friends James and Caroline James. She had refused but did give him 6d so that he could send a telegram to his sister in Cardiff, however when this address was later visited by the police a Mrs Mary Andrews who lived there declared that she not only had never heard of Butler but in fact didn't even have a brother!

The next step was the examination of his clothes by the Monmouthshire public analyst George Thompson. He subsequently found blood on the left sleeve of the shirt and numerous blood spots on the right side of the coat. The right sleeve also bore a jagged cut. Inspector Barry could now connect this cut sleeve with the broken window, surmising that the sharp edges of the glass would have caused it as Butler put his arm through to unlock the door. The fact that the blood spatters on the clothes were all on the right side would perfectly fit the scenario whereby Butler would have entered the bedroom and holding a blunt instrument in his right hand inflicted blows on the recumbent figures.

On Sunday 14th November Butler was taken to the police station in Newport for questioning by Superintendent William Porter. When asked about the stains on his clothes he vehemently denied that they were blood, but instead insisted that they were red paint. A few spots he acknowledged were the result of a cut thumb that had been treated by Elizabeth West during his stay at their house. The replies to Porter's questions were so unsatisfactory that the superintendent decided to immediately charge him with the double murder. Butler now feigned surprise and insisted that he was in bed on the Thursday night and that the Doodys would confirm this.

When Porter explained that Mr and Mrs Doody were in fact unable to support his version of events, Butler flew into a rage shouting, 'They are liars. I went to bed at seven o'clock and went out again at seven the next morning!' The next day he found himself in front of Dr Garrod Thomas in the charge room at Newport County police court. Butler stated proudly that he was 78 years old (sic) and had fought in the Crimean War as if that would exonerate him from all wrongdoing! He was remanded until the Tuesday, the very day that the sad burials of Charles and Mary Thomas took place at Bethesda Chapel cemetery.

Butler was further remanded and during this time he was very busy informing everyone, whether by word of mouth or by letter that the real culprits were the West family as all the evidence pointed to them and not himself. The following letter to a friend was typical of the sort that he sent out:

Please tell me what has happened to Mr and Mrs Doody, as they do not reply to my letter. They know that I did not do the murder as I went to bed at seven o'clock on the night and rose at the same time as she did on the Friday morning, and little Sammy can say the same. As for murdering poor old Charlie Thomas I did not do it. I have done many kind turns for the old man. The people of Basseleg do know who did the murder, and they know it is the Wests ...

The inquest into the murders was resumed at the Tredegar Arms Inn at Basseleg on 26th November when PC Baile was first to give evidence. Mr Rudd the public analyst followed and reported the results of his examination of a number of objects from Tank Cottage. He suggested that the murder weapon was most likely a heavy candlestick holder which bore traces of blood and human tissue. The most crucial piece of information came from the analyst's examination of the wall adjacent to the bed in which the victims lay. This wall was covered with innumerable spots of blood, yet there was a noticeable gap that was free from stains. Rudd was able to demonstrate that this was the position the killer took as he rained blows down on the sleeping couple. These types of blood spots were identical to those found on Butler's coat. Dr Robert Hudson a pathologist totally agreed with this explanation.

After listening to this litany of brutal and sordid facts the jury quickly came to the decision that Thomas Butler was guilty of the murders of Charles and Mary Thomas. He was therefore remanded to the magistrates hearing on 6th December where Mr Harold Pearce represented the Director of Public Prosecutions and Mr E W Pocock, the prisoner. Mr Pearce firstly took up the theme of Butler's changing money fortunes after pointing out that it was well known locally that victims had a quantity of money in their house. Butler had at one time been employed at Tank Cottage as an odd job man and gardener. It also came to light that Charles Thomas had received on the very day he was murdered, two sovereigns, a half sovereign, five florins and a shilling as sick pay. Elizabeth West had stated that when Butler was told to leave her house he still owed them 30 shillings in rent.

His position was further compromised by the evidence given by Elizabeth White who as landlady of a local pub, the Bush Inn told the magistrates that he was a regular customer and on Friday 12th November he had given her a florin for a glass of beer and two bottles of ale. As he was leaving she shouted to him that he had forgotten his change, but he told her to keep it.

Lilian Smith who served at the Great Western Dining Rooms said that Butler on the afternoon of that same Friday had ordered ham and eggs and paid for it with a sovereign plus a tip of one shilling. This was confirmed by Walter Smith, Lilian's husband. When Butler was asked to explain his sudden 'wealth' he told them that he had backed the winner of the Derby at odds of 100-1. However the bookie mentioned by him stated categorically that he had never taken such a bet from the prisoner. With such a weight of overwhelming evidence against him, the magistrates took little time in ruling that Butler should stand trial for murder at the forthcoming Monmouth assizes.

This took place on 23rd February 1910 under Mr Justice Grantham, where the many witnesses came forward to repeat their evidence regarding Butler. After being advised on the various points of law by the judge the jury retired to consider their verdict. It was no great surprise when they returned and the foreman announced that they unanimously found the prisoner guilty of murder. Before Mr Justice Grantham passed sentence Inspector Munroe of Scotland Yard informed the court that Butler had a past criminal record being incarcerated a various times at Gloucester, Brecon, Oxford and Caerleon, mostly for theft.

In addition Munroe continued, he had assumed a number of aliases including George Brown, George Clements, Thomas Palmer and of course Thomas Butler, although his real name was in fact Thomas Clements. After the inspector had finished, Mr Justice Grantham asked the prisoner if he had anything to say before sentence was passed, to which Butler/Clements screamed at the court:

I have not had a fair trial, anything but a fair trial. I consider I have had anything but justice, but you can do what you like, I don't trouble, I think the blood on the jacket could easily be accounted for, I had a cut on the end of my finger and the blood spurted out furiously. The woman who tied it up is in court. I have had no trial - anything but justice. But of course, that is a common thing. You never get justice in this country, but I am not afraid to die and I am not ashamed to live. I am an innocent man. Every witness in this court has told lies.

By now Butler was seething with anger, his face livid as he continued:

*As for old Mrs West, the sneaking old **** and her daughter Florrie ...*

At this point Butler lost complete control of himself and hurled curse after curse on all and sundry; ignoring this the judge donned the black cap and solemnly intoned the death sentence. A violent struggling Butler was then manhandled by police officers from the court. His lawyers lodged an immediate appeal, but on 11th March the appeal judges ruled that the conviction was safe, the execution date being set for Thursday 24th March 1910 at Usk prison. On 22nd March the lawyers for Butler received a letter from the Home Office stating that there would be no reprieve.

As he waited in the condemned cell for the entrance of the executioner on that grey Thursday morning it is difficult to feel any sympathy for Butler. Not only had he brutally killed an elderly couple and stolen money from them, but he had then attempted to place the blame on an entirely innocent family. Did he in fact kill for revenge, just because Florence West had spurned his unwanted advances, or was the revenge angle simply an afterthought?

Whilst Henry Pierrepoint and his assistant John Ellis were pinioning his arms in the condemned cell, Butler turned to John Thorp the prison governor and said, 'You have done all you could for me and I thank you very much.' Strange that

The grave of Charlie and Mary Thomas.

these last words of Butler should be at such odds with all of his previous rantings. Minutes later he was dead.

In the diary of Henry Pierrepoint there is noted an amusing corollary to this case. After the execution he and John Ellis were walking along Maryport Street towards Usk station when they noticed a small crowd of people following a man carrying a suitcase on the opposite side of the road. A small boy suddenly ran up to them and said:

'Do you know who that is?' pointing to the man with the case.

'No,' said Pierrepoint.

'Well,' whispered the boy with suppressed excitement, 'that's the executioner!'

Chapter Eighteen
William Sullivan 1921
'Three suspects, one killer...'

The Llanover Estate occupies a large area of land south of Abergavenny and holds within its boundaries a number of isolated hamlets and villages. One such, Pencroesoped, is practically unknown even to many Monmouthshire born people. However its obliqueness in the history of the county was suddenly torn asunder by the events of 26th October 1921. Lapstone Cottage was home to 60 years old David Thomas and his wife Margaret, twelve years his junior. He was employed as a labourer in a local quarry and like many others at the time eked out a precarious living by rearing their own pigs and chickens.

When David Thomas rose at 6.00am on that cold Wednesday morning it was still dark outside, Margaret dutifully following him downstairs. She prepared a light breakfast for both of them and at about 6.40am he left for work walking the two miles to the quarry. His wife still sat at the kitchen table finishing off her bread and butter together with a strong cup of tea. As a labourer and getting on in years David was glad when five o'clock came so that he could head back home.

Half an hour later he was standing rather puzzled outside of his front door, unable to gain entry as it was locked and he didn't have a key. Although unusual he assumed that his wife had gone out to visit neighbours and hadn't yet returned. He walked around to the back of the house only to find that the pigs hadn't been fed and the chickens were still locked up in the coup. He couldn't see anything through the kitchen window but on retracing his steps to the front he noticed that an upstairs window was ajar. Taking a ladder he climbed up and into the bedroom where he found to his dismay that it appeared to have been ransacked.

In a state of some anxiety he descended the stairs calling out his wife's name but receiving no answer. On entering the kitchen he found the reason why, as lying in a pool of blood on the floor her body partly covered by a mat, was the inert body of Margaret Thomas. There was no doubt that she was dead. As he tentatively approached, his attention was drawn to a bloodstained iron bar lying beside her, obviously the murder weapon. Swaying with shock David Thomas turned and scrambled back upstairs and down the ladder. On landing outside he ran wildly along the road to his neighbour Mrs Evans, and after blurting out what had happened ran on in the direction of the local policeman's house. However before he could reach it he met the district postman who persuaded him to go back to Lapstone Cottage whilst he would go and fetch the police.

Constable Owen Preece eventually arrived at the cottage at around 6.30pm to find a distraught David Thomas waiting outside. They entered together where the police officer confirmed that Thomas's wife was indeed dead. He also noted that the kitchen had been ransacked with the contents of the drawers emptied over the floor. Within half an hour Superintendent John Barry and other officers arrived to take over the investigation. By 9.00pm Dr Thomas Lloyd had examined the body, noting that a quilt had been draped over it extending from the knees to the head. Also a hearthrug was found partly underneath and appeared to have been roughly pulled around the corpse.

This partial covering of Mrs Thomas produced two effects in that the upper portion of the body was still warm whilst the lower uncovered limbs already showed signs of rigor mortis. Dr Lloyd counted eight wounds to the scalp, three to the face and two near the ears. The metal bolt found next to the body was heavily bloodstained and was obviously the weapon used in the attack.

Superintendent Barry also noted that the breakfast things hadn't been removed from the breakfast table, so it was probable that the murderer must have entered the house just after David Thomas had left for work. This might indicate that the murderer had been keeping an eye on the cottage and was waiting for the husband to leave before making his move. Of course Barry also knew that often it was the next of kin who committed murders, so David Thomas could well have killed his wife and then calmly proceeded to walk to the quarry. The superintendent next sent his officers to question neighbours who might have witnessed something unusual or perhaps someone behaving oddly.

Interestingly a number of witnesses told the investigators that they had in fact seen a stranger strolling along the towpath of the nearby Brecon & Newport canal. When David Thomas was told of this he himself remembered that a tramp had called at his house the previous Friday and that his wife had given the caller bread and cheese. The man described by the neighbours appeared to tally with that supplied by Thomas. The next to come forward was George Smith the local milkman who said that he was up and about in the early hours of that Friday morning and had noticed a tramp heading along the towpath towards Abergavenny.

Not only had he seen this tramp but the man had stopped him and holding out an old tin cup asked Smith for a drink of water. He explained that he had journeyed from the workhouse at Newport and hoped to stay that night at the one in Abergavenny. The real significance of Smith's evidence was that the police had found a similar tin cup next to the body in Lapstone Cottage! The milkman continued his narrative saying that on the next day, Saturday 22nd October, he again saw the same man at around 7.00am, but this time he was walking towards Pontypool. Their third meeting took place on the morning that Margaret Thomas was murdered, but at around 5.30am, however Florence the wife of the milkman saw the tramp coming from the direction of Abergavenny some four and a half hours later. She noticed that he was walking very quickly and wearing an overcoat and cap.

In the meantime the police had asked David Thomas to check to see if anything was missing from the cottage. The list he gave them included a navy blue suit, two razors, two watches, a pair of boots and a small quantity of money. Thomas also informed them that his wife had three one pound notes in her jacket and some loose change which he thought was in her purse. The pound notes were still there but the assorted change had been taken. He also added that he had found a pair of old worn boots and a threadbare pair of pyjamas which didn't belong to him. Two days later on the day of the funeral he had occasion to move some furniture upstairs whilst searching for suitable clothes to wear, when he came across a large handkerchief which again wasn't his.

On 28th October an inquest was conducted by a Mr RW Dauncey into the killing which was adjourned until 10th November to give the police more time to investigate the crime. In fact Superintendent Barry had acquired new evidence which apparently indicated that the mysterious tramp went by the name of John Coughlin. He was sixty two years old and as he closely fitted the description given by the witnesses and was seen near the cottage two days after the murder, he was promptly arrested. Coughlin was found to be wearing navy blue trousers similar to those described by the victim's husband. After lengthy questioning at the police station Coughlin was formally charged with carrying out the killing of Margaret Thomas. He made a brief appearance before the magistrates and was remanded for three days.

On Sunday 30th October the funeral of Margaret Thomas took place at Saron Baptist Church in the presence of hundreds of local people, the service being conducted by Rev LC Evans. Afterwards the body of the unfortunate woman was laid to rest in the small adjoining cemetery. It was on the following day that John Coughlin was again brought before the magistrates but in a dramatic turn of events the police admitted that he was innocent and all charges against him were dropped.

Saron Baptist Chapel.

Grave of Margaret Thomas (and later husband David) at Saron Baptist Chapel, Llanover.

This of course was a blow to the investigation so Superintendent Barry now turned his attention to the husband of the deceased, David Thomas. Barry had retraced the journey from Lapstone Cottage to the quarry where Thomas worked so that the time taken could be fairly accurately gauged. He found that it took approximately thirty minutes walking at a reasonable pace this concurring with Thomas's time for completion of the walk home on the day of the murder. However it was found that Thomas had taken twice as long on that particular morning when going to work. His explanation for this discrepancy was that the outward journey was uphill; however a county surveyor was called to disprove this.

No doubt Barry had thought that it was quite possible that Thomas had killed his wife for whatever reason that morning, rifled his own house to make it appear that a robbery had occurred and then calmly walked to work, although forced to set off a little later than usual. In contrast to this, evidence was mounting to suggest that in fact there was another man involved. A neighbour, Mrs Rosser who was a friend of the deceased having occasionally worked at the cottage as a cleaner, now came forward to offer some important information. It seems that Margaret Thomas had been recently upset to find a trail of wet footprints on the path leading up to the cottage and on going around the back she discovered a large man inside their shed. This man mumbled something about collecting dry wood and left immediately.

100

She had discussed this with her husband when he returned from work that evening and suggested to him that it might be safer if they bought a dog as protection. On 24th October two days before her death she had again seen this man but as this time he was on the towpath which was some distance from the house she had ignored it. This evidence by Mrs Rosser did indeed cast a new light on the investigation and Barry slowly became convinced that the husband had nothing to do with his wife's death.

It was not until Thursday 17th November that a firm arrest was made, the man apprehended being a William Sullivan of Cwmbran. He was 41 years of age and had been caught attempting to sell a pair of navy blue serge trousers, later identified by David Thomas as belonging to the missing suit. He was remanded by the magistrates until 18th November and then further remanded until 9th December. At the hearing which took place that day, Mr R Pashley acted for the Director of Public Prosecutions whilst Sullivan was represented by Mr WJ Everett.

The evidence given at this hearing demonstrated why the previous person detained, John Coughlin had been so quickly released. George Smith the milkman had been adamant that Coughlin was not the man he had met. He was also able to confirm that the tin he was offered by the tramp who wanted a drink of water was very distinctly marked and matched the cup found by the body of Margaret Thomas. He immediately identified William Sullivan as that man.

Another witness came forward, a Tudor Evans. He told the inquest that the red and white handkerchief found in Lapstone Cottage appeared to be identical to the one he had seen wrapped around the neck of the accused as there was a distinctive large tear in one corner. Again Florence Smith was able to state that the old boots found in the cottage were very similar to those worn by Sullivan when she saw him on the days before the murder.

Crucially on the actual day of the murder the landlady of the Forge Hammer Inn at Cwmbran, Annie Jones, distinctly remembered Sullivan coming into the pub wearing a pair of almost new boots. She also testified that the accused also appeared to have plenty of money which he spent freely on drinks for himself, Michael his brother and Nick Fellow his brother-in-law. During their stay there Sullivan bought two packs of cigarettes paying for them with a £1 note. Annie Jones also swore that the accused was wearing a blue serge suit.

Further incriminating evidence was given by Richard Groves of 54 Albion Road Pontypool. At about 8.00am on 11th November Sullivan had called at his house, the door being answered by his 14 year old daughter Hannah. Sullivan told her to go and ask her mother if she would like to buy a jacket for 2/6d and a pair of boots for 2/-. Mrs Groves told him to come back later which he did at 6.00pm, but before buying the articles she enquired where he had got them from. He told her that they were given to him by an old lady in part payment for work he had done for her. Satisfied with this explanation Mrs Groves paid him the money.

Two days later Sullivan was there once more, this time asking 3/- for a blue serge waistcoat and trousers, but after some bartering he gave them to Mrs Groves for 2/6d. However by then she had not only heard about the murder but also about some of the stolen articles. She discussed it with Richard her husband and he without hesitation took the boots and clothes to Superintendent Barry at the local police station. Barry sent for David Thomas who on arrival quickly confirmed that they belonged to him although they were by now in a rather worn condition. Barry immediately issued an order for the arrest of William Sullivan who was soon apprehended and brought in for questioning.

There he was asked to account for his movements on both 25th and 26th October. He told them that he had been in the company of another tramp, Frederick Stewart, and that they had travelled to Celynen coke ovens on Tuesday 25th and had left together at 6.00am the next morning, the day Margaret Thomas had been killed. They had walked towards Pontypool but at Hafodyrynys had parted company, he himself going to Cwmbran where he arrived at the Forge Hammer Inn at about noon. Unfortunately this alibi was quickly found to be untrue as when Stewart was interviewed he denied all knowledge of being with Sullivan.

Mr Justice Darling.

Sullivan was now duly charged with the murder for although the evidence was essentially circumstantial, it was truly overwhelming and he duly appeared before Mr Justice Darling at Monmouth Assizes on 7th February 1922. After hearing the evidence given by the many witnesses and the speeches by the prosecution and defence counsels the jury after two and a

THE GOYTRE MURDER.

Cwmbran Man Sentenced To Death.

Pontypool Witness's Vital Evidence.

INFORMATION THAT LED TO SULLIVAN'S ARREST.

half hours retirement, returned to bring in a verdict of guilty. When asked by the judge if he had anything to day before sentence of death was passed, Sullivan replied, 'I am not guilty, and have always said so.' After the prisoner was taken away Mr Justice Darling directed that due praise should be given to Richard Groves, as his coming forward with the stolen clothes was vital to the correct verdict being obtained.

The defence lawyer Bosanquet lodged an appeal on the grounds that the judge had advised the jury unfairly and with bias. The court of appeal led by Mr Justice Avery rejected this, so Bosanquet made an application to the Attorney General. This was again turned down and at 8.00am on Thursday 23rd March

John Ellis and Assistants walking to Usk Prison to hang William Sullivan, 1922.

Crowds outside Usk gaol on the morning of the hanging of Sullivan.

1922 William Sullivan walked to the scaffold at Usk prison where he was hanged by John Ellis and his assistant, Thomas Phillips. His last words as he looked into the eyes of Ellis were, *'I am innocent.'*

William Sullivan proved to be the last man executed at Usk as eight days later the prison was closed down and from then on all hangings were carried out at Cardiff or Swansea.

Staff of Usk Prison at the time of the hanging of William Sullivan in 1922.

PART FOUR

The Hangmen at Usk

*   *   *

Chapter Nineteen
The Hangmen's Tale
'The peace of England and our person's safety, Enforc'd us to this execution?' (Shakespeare)

The epithets 'notorious' and 'infamous' are rarely applied to High Court personnel, whether they are judges, lawyers or members of the juries, yet these same terms have often been reserved for those who have been appointed to carry out court verdicts in cases involving murder. These are the state-appointed executioners. In the age prior to the abolition of the death penalty it was the hangman who was the last to look into the eyes of the prisoners as they stood on the scaffold. It was also the hangmen who have suffered varying degrees of vitriolic abuse by writers on the subject.

All the executions described in this book occurred between 1874 and 1922, so it is interesting to speculate what the general feeling was with regard to hanging during that period. Did it in fact occupy any degree of prominence in society or was the old saying 'an eye for an eye' the order of the day? No census has ever been carried out in this country since the abolition of capital punishment but it would, in my opinion, reveal perhaps a surprising proportion of the population who would

William Calcraft   William Marwood   James Berry   James Ellington   Henry Pierrepoint

John Ellis   Thomas Pierrepoint   Albert Pierrepoint   Harry Allen   Leslie Stewart

The Hangmen of England.

still advocate it for certain types of murder. Certainly when a poll on the subject was conducted in 1953 during the period when abolition was gaining ground in parliament, 73% of the population voted to continue hanging for crimes of murder.

Eyewitness descriptions of executions are none too common, but infrequently a prisoner present in the jail at the time of a hanging has, albeit accidentally, witnessed all or part of the event. One such inmate described the last moments of Samuel Dougal commonly known as the Moat Farm murderer.

> *On the morning of Dougal's execution he spoke no word to anyone. He ate just a small bit of bread, carefully brushed and sponged the suit of private*

clothes in which he was to be executed, and then set to work to pack his kit. He ignored the two warders who were keeping the last vigil with him. I remember hearing the doctor going into his cell that morning, and saying, 'Well, Dougal, how are you?' We were, of course, all locked up in our cells until after the execution, but mine was adjacent to that of Dougal and facing the execution shed at Chelmsford. I could see the whole ceremony through the fanlight. I heard the burial service commenced in Dougal's cell and heard the procession going down the passage. My blood was curdled, but something held me fascinated to the fanlight; I saw two warders, one on each side of the drop.

Samuel Dougal, the Moat Farm Murderer.

The hangman's rope hung from a heavy beam and was looped near the top with a thread of cotton. Dougal very pale and erect walked into the shed followed by the officials. His arms were pinioned and he wore a dark suit. As he took up his position I saw the chaplain close the prayer book, stop reading and stand there very still in his white surplice. A gentleman - the sheriff probably - stood behind the governor and the doctor, who had a watch in his hand. The hangman was a big man. He waited while the chaplain turned to Dougal and said, 'Samuel Dougal, before you are launched into eternity do you say you are guilty of this crime for which you are to suffer?' Dougal hesitated for a fraction of a second. He was right opposite me and I could see his muscles tautening and relaxing round his mouth. Then his lips just moved. 'Guilty,' he murmured. The executioner held Dougal's pinioned hand just a moment and slipped the head-cloth over him, then the noose. I saw the rope jerk and heard a sickening thud. Then I got down feeling nauseated and ill and trembling all over. I never got up to the window again, although there were several executions while I was there.

Stuart Wood was a prisoner at Maidstone when in 1915 George Joseph Smith was hanged. The case involving this notorious killer was given by the newspapers of the day the dramatic title of 'The Brides in the Bath' murders, where Smith drowned three women at different times during 1914 by pushing and holding them under water whilst they took a bath. Wood gave the following account of his hanging.

My cell overlooked the place of executions as did all the other cells on that side and as soon as the staff arrived we were ordered to occupy cells on the ground floor, so that no cell overlooking the scaffold should be occupied. The cell I was put in had to be passed by Smith on the way to the execution ...at Maidstone a condemned prisoner had to walk the whole length of two long halls and at least fifty yards in the open air to reach the scaffold, which is only a few yards from the main gate, a truly terrible ordeal for even the bravest man. Slowly the minutes passed in a silence broken only by the restless pacing of 180 men all tense and excited at the drama proceeding a few yards away. Presently, afar off down the silent halls came the faint shuffle of feet. Nearer and nearer came those halting steps, accompanied by the sound of feet dragging on the flagstones ... as they passed I could hear the laboured breathing of men supporting a heavy burden and a horrible gasping sound as of an animal in the throes of death ... he was in a state of utter collapse. Five minutes passed without a sound. Then, crash! It was all over; George Joseph Smith had gone to join his victims.

To carry out this work required men of a particular type, not fiends nor devils, but men of strong character with an equally strong sense of duty. In this chapter I have penned brief biographies of the four hangmen who undertook the seven executions at Usk prison between 1874 and 1922. They all came from similar working class backgrounds mostly in the north of England, and besides being an occasional 'Servant of His or Her Majesty', had other daily occupations. It would appear that the prison officers at Usk had few qualms over the hangings, except for those who had to endure the stress of being present

either in the condemned cell or on the scaffold. The crowds that gathered outside the prison on the day of each execution seemed to exhibit more a morbid interest in the event rather than being present as a sign of protest.

William Marwood (1818-1883)

William Marwood was by trade a master boot and shoemaker, hailing from Horncastle in Lincolnshire, who had developed a morbid interest in hanging when well into his fifties. At the astonishing age of 54 he carried out his first execution in Lincoln gaol in 1872.

Up until that time the rope used for hanging measured roughly three feet in length. This meant that condemned prisoners often died from strangulation and not from an instantaneous breaking

William Marwood.

of the spinal cord. Marwood, after reading evidence from two surgeons in Ireland, practised what he called the 'long drop' method using a rope of six to ten feet in length. He believed, erroneously, that this would deliver instant death. In fact they still died of asphyxiation but were unconscious at the time. At the least it removed the gruesome spectacle of the 'dancing man'. The current hangman was William Calcraft, now very old and partially crippled by arthritis. Marwood began to correspond with the High Sheriffs and Prison Governors voicing his concerns with regard to Calcraft's technique and standard of performance. The aim he declared was to cause instant death at the end of the 'drop', and that this could only be achieved by taking a scientific approach to the entire process of hanging. Too many times under the longstanding Calcraft had the condemned endured what really amounted to torture as they jerked to and fro at the end of the rope as the life was literally choked out of them. He likewise denounced the oft-repeated comment that 'long, painful and excruciating' deaths were just punishments for these individuals. The sentence of the court was to execute and torture had no part in this procedure.

Marwood's letter to Governor of County Prison, Dundee.

William Marwood, hangman.

This attitude eventually moved the Governor of Lincoln Prison to invite Marwood to carry out an execution employing his 'scientific' principles. In 1871 he duly performed the hanging to the approbation of all the officials present and as a result Marwood now took over the position of chief executioner, Calcraft being brusquely consigned to history. Yet he was also a very shrewd businessman, for although issued with a 2nd class railway ticket when travelling to perform executions, he invariably cashed it in and bought a 3rd class ticket, so pocketing the difference! Against this must be measured his humane approach to hanging and as the inventor of the 'long drop' method he must take his place amongst eminent Victorian pioneers.

Marwood became something of a celebrity with the public at large, his name even entering the lyrics of a popular musical hall song:

> *I'd sooner be a serpent stung,*
> *Or hugg'd by a grizzly bear,*
> *Or crushed by one of Pickford's vans,*
> *Or blown into the air;*
> *I'd sooner be by Marwood hung -*
> *Or slowly fade away,*
> *Than have the least connection*
> *With deceitful Emma Hay.*

However those who were professionally involved with executions were not so enamoured with him. In one of the most perturbing scenes witnessed, the murderer Vincent Walker convulsed and writhed for over seven minutes before he died. In 1880 Marwood committed another poor execution when he hanged William Brownless at Durham gaol. He did encounter a slight problem at Usk prison when he arrived to execute Joseph Garcia as the pit into which the prisoner would fall was waterlogged, this often occurred when the local river was in spate. Much later in 1902 the problem was solved by erecting the gallows on the first floor of the prison - directly opposite the condemned cell. Some thought it poetic justice that the prisoner should witness the assembling of the apparatus of his own death!

Marwood made two visits to Usk, hanging John Henry Gibbs in 1874 and Joseph Garcia in 1878, yet he himself was soon to die after developing pneumonia in September 1883.

James Billington (1847-1901)

Born in Farnworth near Bolton, James Billington became the father of an unusual dynasty of hangmen which included three of his sons. James himself proved to be

James Billington.

an unusual child for instead of playing with toys or playing games with other children, he became fascinated with hanging, even to the extent of carrying out 'executions' on dolls and dummies! On the death of Marwood in 1883 he immediately applied for the post of chief executioner, but as the government had received well over 1,000 applications he was unsuccessful, the job going to a Bartholomew Binns.

Binns however made mistakes and although he was quickly replaced by James Berry, the resourceful Billington was soon appointed to carry out his first execution at Leeds in August 1884. The man he was to execute was a Joseph Laycock who on the way to the scaffold asked Billington if it would hurt. He received the following reassuring reply:

'No, thaal nivver feel it, for thaal be out of existence i' two minutes!'

Billington followed up this execution by writing to the Sheriff at Nottingham requesting that he be allowed to carry out the execution of a man currently on trial there for murder! Billington's letter ended:

'I am a teetotaller ten years and a Sunday school teacher over eight years.'

The request was in vain as the prisoner was found guilty of manslaughter and not murder, so received a jail sentence instead.

Billington was a strong man being at one time a collier and part-time wrestler; he also sang for money in the local pubs, but after signing the pledge remained a teetotaller for the rest of his life. His executions were initially only sited in the north of England as James Berry was the official public hangman, however when Berry himself resigned in 1892 Billington reigned supreme. To this role he brought a rather grotesque aspect in that he invariably wore a black skull-cap when on the scaffold! To his dismay his fame rapidly spread, to the extent that he developed a fear and overwhelming dislike of newspaper reporters especially those who attempted to interview him.

He recorded that when he went to Blackpool in 1892 to attend a friend's wedding

Oscar Wilde.

he was throughout the day literally pursued by the press. His rudeness to them occasioned the local paper to print that Billington would be the last English executioner as capital punishment was soon to be abolished. In fact they had to wait over sixty years before this was finally realised! It was in the same year that he came to Usk to hang Thomas Edwards the murderer of Mary Connolly at Abergavenny. However Billington did achieve some measure of fame when he hanged James Wooldridge at Reading on 7th July 1896 as this was the inspiration for Oscar Wilde's famous poem 'The Ballad of Reading Gaol'. Wilde was himself a prisoner there at the time.

He did not pass in purple pomp
Nor ride a moon white steed,
Three yards of cord and a sliding board,
Are all the gallows need
So with rope of shame the herald came
To do the secret deed.

The last hanging Billington carried out was on 3rd December 1901, the condemned man being a wife-murderer by the name of Patrick McKenna. Strangely Billington knew McKenna by sight as he was also from Bolton. When Billington arrived with Henry Pierrepoint at Strangeways on the day before the execution he was feeling unwell. He was reported as saying that he wished that hadn't come, but the hanging of McKenna was carried out without a hitch the following day.

Within two weeks Billington had succumbed to bronchitis and followed McKenna to the grave. He was just 54 and in his time as executioner he had hanged 147 prisoners.

Henry Pierrepoint (1874-1922)

Henry Albert Pierrepoint, often called Harry, hailed from the village of Clayton near Bradford and was to become the first in line of a new dynasty of hangmen. His brother Thomas and his more famous son Albert, also being engaged as executioners during the twentieth century. He was 25 years old when he decided to write to the Home Secretary expressing his desire to be trained to become an executioner. He received a reply directing him to go to Strangeways Prison for an interview with the Governor Cruikshank. On arrival he was asked what was his business by the gate warder, but feeling rather embarrassed Pierrepoint simply told him he had come for an interview for a prison job. He was given a medical, weighed and had his height measured only to receive a letter a few days later turning him down as he was too short!

He immediately wrote to the Governor who saw the confusion in jobs and sent him back to Newgate for two weeks training. As soon as the authorities had verified that he was of good and sound character Pierrepoint's name was added to the official list of those empowered to carry out executions. His first appointment was cancelled owing to the prisoner being granted a

Henry Pierrepoint demonstrating pinion straps for one armed man.

last-minute reprieve but in 1901 he was given the job of acting as an assistant to James Billington when the latter hanged Marcel Faugeron at Newgate. Legend has it that immediately after Faugeron dropped through the trapdoors the attending prison doctor took Pierrepoint's pulse and exclaimed, 'You'll do!'

Henry Pierrepoint was now kept very busy in his role of assistant hangman to both James and William Billington. Eventually however he began to carry out executions himself and would later write, 'I was very ambitious for duty and loved my work on the scaffold'. In fact by 1905 he was the No. 1 hangman and held this position until around 1910 when John Ellis appeared to succeed him. Pierrepoint subsequently developed a dislike bordering on hatred for the new man once remarking rather theatrically that, 'If I ever meet Ellis I'll kill him - it doesn't matter if it is in the church!' This rivalry based presumably on jealousy was to eventually have catastrophic consequences for Pierrepoint.

On 18th July 1910, just a mere 4 months after hanging William Butler at Usk he travelled to Chelmsford prison to execute Frederick Foreman for the brutal murder of Elizabeth Ely. She was the girlfriend of Foreman and lived with him in a disused railway carriage that lay rusting in a field at Wennington. Her battered body was found near a footpath which traversed the field, all the evidence pointing to Foreman as her killer. The jury agreed and he was found guilty and sentenced to death. On the afternoon prior to the day of execution Pierrepoint arrived at the prison obviously under the influence of drink. Unfortunately his assistant on that occasion was John Ellis who quietly remonstrated with him, offering the

Executioners Henry Pierrepoint and John Ellis on their way to a hanging.

advice that being in such a condition would give a damaging impression of the role of the hangman.

All the old smouldering jealousies suddenly came to the surface and Pierrepoint screamed a tirade of abuse at Ellis before launching an attack which resulted in his assistant being knocked to the floor. A warder named Nash arrived and attempted to calm Pierrepoint down but the raging hangman managed to land another blow to the side of Ellis's head. After regaining control of the situation the prison staff ensured that there would be no further trouble between the two men and the following morning the execution went off without a hitch. However the incident was reported to the appropriate authorities by the prison Governor and Pierrepoint's name was subsequently taken off the list. A sad exit for a man who during his career had brought and developed a range of improving techniques to the process of hanging.

John Ellis (1874-1932)

A number of authors have commented on the potentially dehumanising effect that hanging has on the executioners themselves. Perhaps this is best illustrated in the case of John Ellis. Although he was an official executioner for nearly 23 years he was prone to both anxiety and stress at every execution he carried out. During his time he hanged many of the most-notorious criminals in British legal history, including Dr Hawley Crippen, Major Herbert Armstrong the Hay poisoner, Edith Thompson, George Smith the 'Brides in the Bath' murderer, and the accused spy Sir Roger Casement.

As with a later hangman Albert Pierrepoint, Ellis saw his job as a sacred duty where the primary object was to carry out the execution as quickly as possible. The often sordid events that finally placed the prisoner on the scaffold was of no concern to him, his duty was to inflict as little suffering as possible at the hanging. He was by all accounts a mild mannered man in domestic life, employed as a barber in Rochdale, but he did have a profound sense of duty and would react sharply if he felt that there was any interference from prison officials. During the hours leading up to an execution he would

John Ellis Executioner.

continually check and re-check every detail to ensure that everything went smoothly. William Billington once remarked that Ellis, '... *wur alus nervous and worried that all wur alreet.'*

His career got off to a rather ignominious beginning when he rather naively gave an interview to a newspaper reporter. As a result of this he wasn't for a period of time given any assignments by the commissioners, this had the effect of causing him to become not only reclusive but extremely reticent about the work he undertook. One aspect of his job, which haunted him throughout his time as an executioner was his abhorrence of hanging women as he firmly believed that their sentences of death should always be commuted to life imprisonment. The famous case of Edith Thompson was peculiarly distressing for him.

Edith Thompson.

She and her lover were found guilty of murdering her husband and although it was the lover who carried out the deed, Edith was convicted of aiding and abetting. Ellis along with many in the public domain mistakenly believed that she would be reprieved, however her appeal was eventually turned down. When he arrived at the condemned cell on the morning of the execution she was in a state of near collapse requiring two female warders to get her to her feet. Ellis himself was unnerved by her pitieous condition as they carried her semi-conscious form to the scaffold and so to her death.

John Ellis came to Usk prison with his two assistants on 23rd March 1922 when he executed William Sullivan for the murder of Margaret Thomas. It was the last ever hanging there and the prison itself was temporarily closed a few days later. It was on 10th October

Public demonstration by John Ellis.

of the following year that he hanged a second woman, Susan Newell at Glasgow followed by John Eastwood at Leeds before tendering his resignation to the Prison Commissioners. In his career he had assisted at 43 executions and hanged 134 murderers over a period of 22 years.

Personal tragedy was to follow as over the next few years his profession as a barber began to fail and he started drinking heavily. In the throes of depression he attempted unsuccessfully to take his own life but after a stern warning from a local magistrate he appeared to regain himself. However on 20th September 1932, after threatening his family, he cut his throat with a razor. Over a hundred people attended his funeral in Balderstone, but no one appeared on the day to represent his former employers, the prison commissioners.

Epilogue
'Cap, Noose, Pin, Lever, Drop...'

In the era stretching from the early 1930s up to the mid 1950s, one name was to become central to judicial hanging, that of Albert Pierrepoint. The son of Henry and nephew of Thomas, both hangmen, he was not only the most prolific executioner of the twentieth century but also the most proficient. He hanged many of Britain's most infamous murderers together with over 200 Nazi war criminals found guilty at the Nuremburg trials.

Albert Pierrepoint No.1 hangman 1932-1956.

In 1947 responding to growing concerns within Parliament, the post-war Labour government set up a Royal Commission under Sir Ernest Gowers to review all aspects of capital punishment. In 1949 they asked Pierrepoint to give evidence before them. He was not particularly happy about this as his work was secretive in the extreme, hidden away from the public at large, witnessed by only a select few, its workings never divulged for general consumption. In fact the public's only knowledge of his work was through the dulcet tones of the BBC wireless announcer Alva Liddell who would, during the early news bulletin, state in an appropriately serious voice that, 'so and so had been executed at so and so prison at 8 o'clock this morning!'

However the Commission did receive the following Home Office Memorandum regarding the course to be followed after a conviction for murder. Today its contents are no longer governed by the Official Secrets Act as it was then:

Immediately a prisoner sentenced to death returns from court, he is placed in a cell for condemned prisoners and is watched day and night by two officers. Amenities such as cards, chess, dominoes etc., are provided in the cell and the officers are encouraged to - and in fact invariably do - join the prisoner in these games.

Newspapers and books are also provided. Food is supplied from the main prison kitchen, the prisoner being placed on hospital diet, with such additions as the medical officer considers advisable. A pint of beer or stout is supplied daily on request and ten cigarettes or half an ounce of pipe tobacco are allowed unless there are medical reasons to the contrary. The prisoner may smoke in his cell and exercise.

It is the practice for the Governor, medical officer and chief officer to visit a prisoner under sentence of death twice daily, and the chaplain or minister of any other denomination has free access to him.

He may be visited by such of his relations, friends and legal advisers as he desires to see and as are authorised to visit him by the Visiting Committee, and he is given special facilities to write and receive letters.

The executioner and his assistant arrive at the prison by 4p.m. on the day preceeding the execution, and are not permitted to leave the prison until the execution has been carried out.

They see the prisoner at exercise and test the execution apparatus with a bag of sand approximately of his weight. The bag is left hanging overnight to stretch the rope.

It is common practice for the Governor to visit a prisoner before he retires for the night to talk to him and give him an opportunity to say anything he may wish.

On the morning of the execution it is usual for the chaplain to spend the last hour with the prisoner and remain with him until the execution is over.

Some 20 minutes before the time fixed for the execution the High Sheriff, or more usually the Under Sheriff, arrives at the prison, and a few minutes before it is due, proceeds with the Governor and medical officer to the place of execution.

The executioner and assistant wait outside the condemned cell, with the chief officer and officer detailed to conduct the prisoner to the execution chamber. On a signal given by the Sheriff they enter and the executioner pinions the prisoner's arms behind his back. He is escorted to the drop with one officer on either side. The Sheriff, the Governor and the medical officer enter the execution chamber directly by another door.

The prisoner is placed on the drop on a marked spot so that his feet are directly across the division of the trap doors. The executioner places a white cap over the prisoner's head and places the noose around his neck, while the assistant pinions his legs. When the executioner sees that all is ready he pulls the lever.

The medical officer at once proceeds to the pit and examines the prisoner to see that life is extinct. The shed is then locked and the body hangs for one hour. The inquest is held the same morning.

Burial of the body takes place in the prison graveyard during the dinner hour. The chaplian reads the burial service.

Not suprisingly after a period of four years gestation, the Royal Commission's report produced nothing but equivocation on the subject!

A recent book offering an otherwise excellent exposition of the history of judicial hanging is somewhat marred by its final chapter where the author launches into a veritable tirade against capital punishment. Indeed he reserves his most emotive diatribes for the hangmen themselves who in his opinion generally occupy a lower order of humanity than those whom they executed. This is at best disingenuous and at worst palpable nonsense. Are we to believe that Albert Pierrepoint was a lesser human being than for example, Irma Grese who deliberately set half-starved dogs on the Jewish prisoners at Auschwitz concentration camp, or Josef Kramer the 'Beast of Belsen', Haigh the 'Acid Bath Murderer, John Christie who killed and walled up eight women at 10 Rillington Place, or more recently Harold Shipman who clinically dispatched hundreds of his patients.

Again the argument is put forward that executioners such as Pierrepoint didn't have to hang anyone, which is of course quite true, in the same way that the prosecuting counsels didn't have to prosecute or a High Court Judge didn't have to become a judge. When the juries returned guilty verdicts on murderers these Officers of the Law knew exactly what the penalty would be. It didn't deter them because it was the law of the land, the same law which is made in Parliament by those we democratically elect. This is not a plea for the return of the death penalty, although 218 MPs did vote for that in 1988, but perhaps to recognise the socio-philosophical thinking of the time. Judicial hanging will almost certainly never again appear on the Statute Book in Britain, yet there are certain instances such as the Ian Huntley case that does make one ponder on what really is the correct punishment for such evil acts.

Of course the process of hanging is barbaric, but so is the act of murder that placed the convicted killer on the scaffold in the first place. In the Llangibby murders described in Part Two of this book where father and mother had their throats cut, three of their children suffering similar knife wounds and in addition being partly burned, I suspect at the time little thought was spent on the inhumanity of the hangman or the 'unjust' fate of the culprit who died at the end of a rope.

Abolitionists often employ the theme that executions don't allow the possibility of reforming the character of the prisoner, so that on release they are able too take a normal role in society. Yet Myra Hindley who was convicted with Ian Brady in 1966 for the infamous 'Moors Murders' had her original sentence repeatedly extended by successive ministers. Still incarcerated she died of a heart attack aged 60 in 2002. Conversely the proposition that hanging was an effective deterrent to homicide is demonstrably undermined by the 450 plus hangings carried out over a

Myra Hindley.

period of 24 years by Albert Pierrepoint. He himself wrote in his autobiography, 'Executioner Pierrepoint' published in 1974:

It is said to be a deterrent. I cannot agree. There have been murders since the beginning of time, and we shall go on looking for deterrents until the end of time.

He also added:

I have come to the conclusion that executions achieve nothing.

However in a BBC radio interview some two years later he retracts this point of view when expressing his concern at the increase of the crime in modern Britain.

The reasoning that life is held more cheaply because of judicial executions has also proved to be false; over four decades have passed since its abolition, yet it is unfortunately true that life *has* become cheaper.

Of course the word 'cheap' is more often mentioned in its financial connotation, especially in the arguments that surround contemporary sentencing for murder. It has been estimated that the current cost of maintaining a prisoner is around £35,000 per annum, so for a single individual serving a life sentence of 50 years this would equate to an outlay of well over a million and a half pounds. Those in favour of a return to hanging emphasise the fiscal disparity between carrying out an execution and that of longterm imprisonment. The loosening of the hangman's noose has produced a similar effect on the strings of the public purse.

Biblical references can be utilised by both pro-and anti-abolitionists as *an eye for an eye* vies with *thou shalt not kill*. In the final analysis it comes down to a matter of revenge by society, with the inherent concept that a killer has lost the right to walk this earth. In this it must be borne in mind that we are discussing Capital *Punishment*, and not its role as a deterrent.

Although the Abolition of Capital Punishment became law in 1965, there did remain a number of crimes that in theory still carried the death penalty, amongst them being treason, the murder of a police officer and piracy. To cover this possibility, however remote, a working execution chamber was maintained at Wandsworth Prison until the then Home Secretary Jack Straw repealed this cause in 1999. During this period Harry Allen who had succeeded Pierrepoint as chief executioner in 1956, remained on stand-by, awaiting the call that never came. He was a lifelong supporter of capital punishment, being of the opinion that since its abolition society's discipline had catastrophically declined. Allen passed away aged 80 in 1992. The last executions in Britain took place at 8am on 13th August 1964 when Harry Allen hanged Gwynne Owen Evans at Strangeways, whilst Peter Anthony Allen was executed at the very same moment by assistant hangman Robert Stewart at Walton Prison; Evans and Allen had callously killed a 53 year old laundry man, John West, during the course of an armed robbery.

As all the participants in this controversial story are now themselves dead, so the dust of their actions has settled with the passing of time, it is left as always for history to ultimately offer its judgement. In the final analysis it is worth reflecting on the words of Lord Denning with which I opened this book, for without doubt the arguments for and against judicial execution will forever be debated as long as humans slay humans.

Epitaph

To Hang a Man

To hang a man:
To fit the cap,
And fix the rope,
And let him drop.
I know, I know:
What can you do!
You have no choice,
You're driven to;
You can't be soft -
A man like that:
But Oh it seems -
I don't know what -
To hang a man!

(Ralph Hodgson)

Bibliography

Books
Stewart P. Evans: Executioner. The Chronicles of James Berry (2004)
Brian Bailey: Hangmen of England (1989)
I. Bale: Through Seven Reigns. A History of Newport Police (1960)
Charles Fairfield: Some Account of George William Wilshire, Baron Bramwell (1898)
P. Fuller & B. Knapp: Welsh Murders Vol. 1 (1986)
Roger Williams: Their Deadly Trade (2004)
Jan Barrow: From Dawn till Dusk (2004)
Keith Watkins: The Llangibby Murders. *Abersychan & Garndiffaith LHG* (2004)
Simon James: The Llangibby Murders: A New Theory. *Gwent FHS* (March 2002)
E.A. Williams: Open Verdict (1967)
Justin Atholl: Shadow of the Gallows (1954)
Arthur Machen: The Chronicle of Clemendy (1925)
J H Clark: Usk Past and Present (n.d.)
David R. Lewis: Early Victorian Usk (1982)
Philip Priestley: Victorian Prison Lives
Geoffrey Best: Mid-Victorian Britain 1851-75 (1985)
J. Preece & T. Phillips: House of Correction. Usk Prison. Part 1 (1993)
Brian Foster: The Usk Houses of Correction. *Gwent Local History Journal* (94/2003)
John Ellis: Diary of a Hangman (1996)
Esme Lucas Weare: Another World (2005)
Doris E Long: Coed-y-paen & Llangibby Past and Present (n.d.)
Joseph Bradney: A History Of Monmouthshire. Volume 3 Part 1 (1923)
Olive Phillips: Monmouthshire (1951)
Terry Underwood: Foul Deeds & Suspicious Deaths Around Newport (2005)
Newport Corporation: The Newport Pictorial (1998)
Steve Fielding: Pierrepoint: A Family of Executioners (2006)

Newspapers and Journals
Star of Gwent 19 July 1874
Usk Gleaner: 1878
South Wales Argus: 2 September 1947
Western Mail: 19 November 1878
Pontypool Free Press: 1892
Monmouthshire Merlin and South Wales Advertiser: 19 July and 1 November 1878
County Observer & Monmouthshire Central Advertiser 20
Monmouthshire Beacon: 15 April 1977
Gwent Police Journal: 1985
Hereford Times: 27 July 1878

Public Record Documents
Joseph Garcia Home Office File HO 9464/75796
Assize Depositions ASSI 6/16
Microfiche Census Information Newport Reference Library
Census England and Wales (Monmouthshire) 1841

Acknowledgements

I must firstly offer special thanks to my long suffering wife Wendy, whose entreaties to me to spend more time on our garden often fell on deaf ears!

I would also like to express my gratitude and thanks to the following, whose help and kindness contributed so much to the making of this book:

Mr Marcus Brown, Arthur Griffiths, David Husband, Pat Jones, David Lewis, Jenny Mee, Penny Nicholas, Janet Pollock, John Evans, Sian Hayward, Staff of Chepstow, Newport and Usk Libraries, Staff of Gwent Record Office, The Rural Life Museum Usk.

Special thanks to Dr Matt Hayward for undertaking the onerous task of proof reading, to Peter Lavin for his oft-needed computer skills, and to Glen Roderick who kindly provided me with historical documents from Usk Prison.